Motorbooks International Illustrated Buyer's Guide Series

Illustrated

PACKARD
BUYER'S ★ GUIDE™

All Packard Cars and Commercial Vehicles, 1899 to 1958

Richard M. Langworth

Motorbooks International
Publishers & Wholesalers

To the memory of Dick Teague,
and to Packard enthusiasts worldwide

First published in 1991 by Motorbooks International Publishers & Wholesalers, P O Box 2, 729 Prospect Avenue, Osceola, WI 54020 USA

Motorbooks International books are also available at discounts in bulk quantity for industrial or sales-promotional use. For details write to Special Sales Manager at the Publisher's address

Library of Congress Cataloging-in-Publication Data
Langworth, Richard M.
    Illustrated Packard buyer's guide / Richard Langworth.
        p.   cm.—(Motorbooks International illustrated buyer's guide series)
    ISBN 0-87938-427-1
    1. Packard automobile—Purchasing.   2. Packard automobile—Collectors and collecting.   I. Title.   II. Series.
TL215.P25L36 1991
629.222'2—dc20   90-24615

On the front cover: A beautiful 1941 Darrin One-Eighty convertible Victoria owned by Ralph Marano. *Bud Juneau*

On the back cover: A 1934 Model 1108 Twelve diesel (top) and a Super Clipper convertible (bottom) by Derham of Rosemont, Pennsylvania.

Printed and bound in the United States of America

Contents

Acknowledgments

It may seem natural that after sixteen years of editing and publishing *The Packard Cormorant* magazine I am considered a logical person to add Packard to Motorbooks International's Illustrated Buyer's Guide series. But Packard is a daunting subject for any author. Indeed, when I conceived and planned the *Automobile Quarterly* marque history, *Packard: A History of the Motorcar and the Company* back in 1974, I hired more than twenty different authors and contributors. My personal experience with the cars is limited. I have owned only two: a 1948 Custom Eight named *Fat Albert* and a 1953 Patrician repainted a shocking pink, whose thirst for gas was matched only by its granitic durability.

What I can offer is the experience of having dealt with hundreds of far more knowledgeable and serious Packard people who have contributed to the magazine over the years, whose names are too numerous to be mentioned here, although many will be found in the notes, appendices and other references.

This book would be much less than it is without the collaboration and advice of my friend George Hamlin, past master Packardian and for sixteen years senior editor of *The Packard Cormorant*. Hamlin wrote 95 percent of the Problem Areas material and the chapter on professional cars and trucks; he was the source of wise suggestion and criticism throughout.

I should like also to thank Greg Field, Michael Dregni, Barbara Harold, the editorial staff of Motorbooks International and the countless members of the various Packard clubs who provided information and experiences.

Introduction

This Illustrated Buyer's Guide covers every model from the 1899 Packard Model A to the final 1958 models not because they're all available (far from it), but because I thought they all deserved consideration.

Buying Packards is now largely a matter of opportunity: You may set out seeking the elegant 1947 Custom Super Clipper limousine, but settle for a mint-condition 1948 Custom Eight or 1950 Super Deluxe sedan because its price or condition make it impossible to pass up. You can count single-cylinder Packards on one, maybe two hands—but that doesn't mean another one might not surface tomorrow. In areas with a wide choice—Patricians or One Twentys, for example—I have tried to channel my comments so as to cover the pros and cons of various models and years from the standpoint of collector esteem, their value as cars, their ability to hold up, their frequency of appearance and, particularly, what a good one is going to cost you.

Chapters otherwise follow the Illustrated Buyer's Guide series' format: a background (but not a marque history); remarks on what to look for, such as condition, special models, peculiar maladies, and explanations of differences between various models; problem areas; production figures by model year; identification notes; specifications; and price history.

For statistics I acknowledge four excellent sources: the National Auto Dealers Association and Red Book used car value guides published over the years from 1932 to date; *Packard: A History of the Motorcar and the Company*, which I had the privilege to structure and coedit; the *Standard Catalog of American Cars 1805–1942* and the *Standard Catalog of American Cars 1946–1975* (see the Publications section at the end of this book).

Price History

Value guides are controversial subjects among collectors. Some believe that cars should never be represented in print by columns of filthy lucre, that dollar values have no place in old-car publications. Others insist that price and value are intrinsic to the subject and cannot be ignored.

I had to wrestle with this moral dilemma three years ago when I was asked to become editor of a financial newsletter on collector cars, *Automotive Investor*. I finally decided that collectors who ignore the financial aspect do so at their peril. The press of time forced me to give up the editorship of that newsletter in 1990, but I don't feel any differently about the subject: Whatever the mistakes of the old-car publishing industry in the past, money simply cannot be ignored if one expects to be knowledgeable about the cars.

As enthusiasts, we primarily love the vehicles in their own right and are not interested in parlaying them into profits as we would a stock portfolio. But the days when we owned a lot of cars and played with them all for relatively little money are over. Today the collector car "hobby" is in reality a big business. The typical old-car collection has shrunk dramatically, and the "entry level" is so forbidding that many of us can afford only one car.

Whether we are one-car collectors or owners of stables, however, we have to take notice of the financial angle and be able to distinguish honest value from dishonest hype. Any Illustrated Buyer's Guide worthy of the name owes it to its readers to say what a car is worth, and where it has been in terms of value, as a permanent reference point.

Thus I decided to present here the price history of top-condition, show-quality cars over the past decade—specifically, the approximate high price of each model in 1982, 1987 and 1992. Also, from my experience with *Automotive Investor*, I have calculated the compound annual rate of return on those figures, as if they'd been invested in a certificate of deposit or a stock portfolio instead of a car.

For example, if you bought a Caribbean in prime condition for $10,000 in 1982 and it was worth $30,000 in 1992, that represents a compound return rate of 24.6 percent, which is pretty good by 1992 interest rates.

The use of such strict calculations requires qualifications. First, cars are not certificates of deposit or stock portfolios; they require maintenance, insurance, parts and service. The return rates listed in this text do not account for upkeep, repairs and running costs. Second, the price figures are highly arbitrary, taken from three or four sources and averaged. Third, prices apply only to very fine, over-ninety-five-point (on the traditional 0–100–point scale of show judging) cars in original or restored condition, which always command far more than the same models in mediocre condition. Finally, excellent cars regularly sell quietly and privately for prices dramatically *below* the "highs" cited; conversely, the occasional example may sell for a lot more at a loudly trumpeted auction.

It is not possible to measure the individual overhead costs involved in eight years' ownership of any specific car, although obviously, running costs and insurance are going to be higher for a 1933 Twelve, say, than a 1952 Clipper. On the other hand, the "compound rate of return" does not take into consideration the intangible fun of ownership, which after all counts for something.

I like to say to myself that the cost of maintenance, insurance, garaging and so on is evenly balanced by the fun of ownership, so the two factors cancel each other out. This is perhaps too glib a statement—but it does point to a salient fact: The return figure is only a comparative guide to what the best examples of each model sold for from 1982 to 1992. Where the car is going in the future

is up to you to decide, based on your own perceptions of the market.

Rating System

I so enjoyed Graham Arnold's *Illustrated Lotus Buyer's Guide* that I determined to structure this book, as I did the previous *Illustrated Studebaker Buyer's Guide*, along the same lines. Arnold made his book entertaining, a work to be enjoyed by the nonspecialist as well as the marque nut. I have tried to do that, and have thus substituted his three-way rating system of Fun, Investment and Anguish for the simpler star ratings found in most other series books. Under each category I have assigned a number from 1 (lowest) to 10 (highest).

It occurred to me that the Illustrated Buyer's Guide series' traditional one- to five-star rating system was fairly imprecise, not broadly indicative of a car's character. A 1929 Packard Speedster Eight is great fun and a prime investment, for example, and would get five stars in the old system. However, finding certain parts will be nearly impossible, and a star rating would not reveal this; a high figure in the Anguish column would be more suggestive. On the other hand, more conventional classic Packards rate much lower numbers for Anguish and almost as high figures for Fun and Investment.

Arnold defined his Anguish factor as reflecting two aspects of ownership: "First, the likelihood of outright failure and frequency of nagging faults; and second, the shortage of spare parts and/or information, even sympathy." I have adopted that definition wholesale. Of course, mechanical anguish is not a common problem with Packards of any era because they were so well built to begin with.

Arnold's rating system remains imprecise, as all rating systems do, but it's far more revealing than one to five stars. I liked it, and I hope you will find it useful.

Richard M. Langworth
Hopkinton, New Hampshire
October 1991

One- and Two-Cylinder Models, 1899–1903

Models A, B, C, F and G

	Fun	Investment	Anguish
Models A, B, C and F	8	2	9
Model G	8	8	10

J. Ward Packard, who with his brother William Doud, founded the Warren, Ohio, company and served as its first president, built his first cars using the simple, sound principles he had learned from the school of experience with other people's horseless carriages. The multiauthor book *Packard: A History of the Motorcar and the Company* contains a fascinating, blow-by-blow account of Packard Motor Car Company's development, written by the leading researcher of the Warren era, Terry Martin. Based in part on the Packard brothers' diaries, Martin's work is strongly recommended to collectors interested in this period.

Among the new facts brought out by Martin was that five, not one, of the initial Model As were built, although all were considered preproduction prototypes in one form or another. Packard's first industry first, the H-pattern gearshift, was installed on the first Model A. Alas, only one of these historically priceless cars is known today, in the collection of Lehigh University, J. Ward Packard's alma mater.

The Model B, announced in early 1900, was the first true production Packard, with a run of forty-nine units. Only one body style was used, an open runabout mainly designed for one person, although a passenger could be carried facing the rear using the other

The most famous Packard Single, *Old Pacific*, which crossed North America in 1903. It was recently restored for the Henry Ford Museum by Terry Martin. *Henry Ford Museum*

side of the driver's backrest. Automatic spark advance and foot pedal throttle control were notable features.

The Model B continued in production briefly during 1901, but the leading Packard by then was the Model C, the first model with a steering wheel instead of a tiller, another first later claimed by the company. Against the 9 hp of the B, the C offered 12 hp, and passengers could now be carried facing either forward or to the rear. This model sold for $1,500.

Packard's Models D and E were experimental, so the next production version was the 1902 Model F, immortalized in 1903 by Tom Fetch in his epic transcontinental journey. Fetch used a 1903 model known as *Old Pacific*, which, recently restored by Terry Martin, may be seen at the Henry Ford Museum in Dearborn, Michigan. *Old Pacific* demonstrated what we might call Packard's

first facelift: the sloping, Renault-style hood installed on all Fs that year. It also had a slightly longer wheelbase than did the 1902 model.

The Model F used a Model C drivetrain but was evolving rapidly as the horseless carriage became more civilized and practical. Instead of spindly wire wheels it had wooden artillery wheels; instead of a primitive planetary transmission, it had a three-speed selective sliding gear arrangement. As in the earlier single-cylinder models, drive was by chain; hand and foot brakes operated on the rear wheels.

Packard also built a two-cylinder car, the unlamented Model G, powered by two single-cylinder engines mounted in tandem, each with its own carburetor. Only four of these relatively huge cars were built, and none are known to survive. Finding one would be an important achievement for any

A Model C, as advertised in *The Horseless Age*, October 1900, was the first Packard with a steering wheel. Few exist today.

collector. Model Gs weighed about 4,000 lb., a lot to move around, even with double the power of the Model F.

What To Look For

Only a handful of single-cylinder Packards exist in the United States, and some of these have been built up from far-flung parts, the bodies pieced together from scratch. Although the cars are simple in operation, running one requires an intimate knowledge of mechanics, not to mention a close acquaintanceship with Terry Martin (see the Parts and Services section at the end of this book). Martin is also most likely to know where any single-cylinder Packards may be found. They are so scarce that your only choice will most likely be a Model F.

Problem Areas

Parts, particularly body parts, are the chief difficulty. Virtually all body components that are missing will have to be built from scratch; damaged parts should be restored rather than replaced with wholly new replicas. Single-cylinder engines do not defy competent mechanics with experience in similar powerplants, but no two-cylinder engines are known to exist.

The Model F was most typically encountered in runabout form, with "painting and upholstering to suit customers' tastes." Acetylene gas headlamps and spotlight were accessories.

Artist's rendering of Charles Schmidt driving the Model F *Gray Wolf* racer, shows the spare bodywork of competition cars from the dawn of the motoring age. *Charles Betts, Jr.*

Production

Model	Total	Model	Total
A	5	F	179
B	49	G	4
C	81		

Serial Numbers

Early Packards were numbered in the order built.

Identification

Models A and B: Tiller steering, full-elliptic rear springs, single-cylinder gas engine, chain drive, wire wheels.

Model C: Steering wheel, cycle fenders, wire wheels, twin Dietz oil sidelamps.

Model F: Wooden artillery wheels; twin acetylene headlamps as well as Dietz oil sidelamps.

Model G: Two cylinders.

Specifications

Model	Cylinder	Bore x Stroke	CI	Bhp	Wheelbase
A, B, C	1	6.0 x 6.5 in.	183.8	9	76 in.
F	1	6.0 x 6.5	183.8	12	84
G	2	6.0 x 6.5	367.6	24	91

Chassis and drivetrain: Solid axles with full-elliptic leaf springs front and rear and solid tires. Models A, B and C: Chain drive with two speeds forward and reverse. Models F and G: Three speeds forward. Curb weight 1,500 lb. on Models A, B and C; 1,750 lb. on Model F; 4,000 lb. on Model G.

Bodies: Runabout with optional dos-a-dos seats (passengers face forward and backward) on Models A, B and C; Surrey-runabout and rear tonneau model was offered on Model F.

Price History

95+ point condition 1	1982	1987	1992	Return*
Model F	$50,000	$55,000	$60,000	3.7%

*Compound annual rate of return for comparison purposes only, based strictly on high average prices unadjusted for upkeep, repairs and running costs.

Chapter 2

Fours, 1904–1912

Models K, L, N, 24 (Model S),
30 (Model U) and 18 (Model NA)

	Fun	Investment	Anguish
Model K	6	6	10
Models L and N	7	7	8
Model 24 and 30	8	5	8
Model 18	6	4	8

The four-cylinder Packards established the marque as a luxury car just short of the highest echelon—Locomobile, Pierce, Peerless—which Packard finally joined with the 1912 Six. The Fours also established one or two Packard design hallmarks that survived, in one way or another, through the final Packards in 1958: the hexagon motif of the hubs on the 1906 Model S and the ox-yoke-shaped radiator grille with cusps flanking a curved top section on the 1904 Model L. Packard Fours were and are the ultimate brass models, veritably laden with the shiny stuff. After the Six arrived, Packard opted for a more conservative image and substituted many black-painted areas for brass.

First of the series was the 1903 Model K, priced at $7,000 in 1903, comparable to two or three Rolls-Royce Corniches in 1992. The K achieved more Packard firsts, establishing the front-engine, rear-drive configuration and the four-speed gearbox.

President Henry Joy—who succeeded J. Ward Packard at the time of the company's move from Warren, Ohio, to Detroit, Michigan, in 1903—hated the Model K for its unreliability. But Chief Engineer Charles Schmidt successfully raced a K-based *monoposto*, turning the flying mile at nearly 80 mph at Ormond-Daytona Beach.

Fours were produced to the exclusion of single-cylinder models starting in 1904, when Packard introduced the much-im-

Symbolic of Packard's great Fours is the first of the breed, the 1904 Model L restored by Dick Teague and now on display at the Henry Ford Museum. *Henry Ford Museum*

Wicker hampers and golf bag container were owner's accessories on the Ford Museum Model L. Entry to the rear of the tonneau body was through the rear door. *Henry Ford Museum*

Brass acetylene lamps were standard on all Packard Fours; the Model L's were made by Gray & Davis of Amesbury, Massachusetts. Originals, now in demand as room lights, are scarce and expensive today. *Henry Ford Museum*

proved Model L, which sold over 200 units, more than any previous model. The L would cruise at a heady 35 mph, but it was cannily downpriced to just $3,000 by the company, which was girding now for serious sales competition.

In 1905 the Model L was replaced by the Model N, offered in a wider selection of bodies including brougham and limousine. The N doubled the production run of the L. The slightly larger engine of the N was the basis of the later Model NA, better known as the 18.

Volume doubled again with the 1906 Model S or, as Packard now began calling its cars, 24, named for its brake horsepower. Developed by Schmidt, the 24 featured a new T-head engine and magneto ignition, components that Packard would use through the early Sixes.

From 1907 through 1912, the largest Packard was the Model U or 30, again numbered for its horsepower. The 30 was a majestic car that evolved into the shape everyone recognized from afar as Packard's own. With a run of almost 10,000 units, the 30 was by far the most popular Packard to date, and offered in a wide variety of open and closed body styles. These bodies were interchangeable, so many owners had two: an open style for summer and a closed version for the colder months.

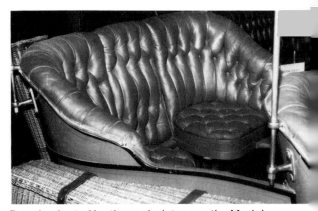

Deeply pleated leather upholstery on the Model L was standard equipment. Note the bulb horn to the right of the steering column. *Henry Ford Museum*

The 30 was joined in 1909 by the aforementioned 18 or Model NA, priced $1,000 less, carrying the 262 ci engine and mounted on shorter wheelbases. The 18 was an attempt to expand Packard's market downward, but by then, the typical customer preferred the big 30, and that model took the lion's share of sales.

What To Look For

The magnificent Packard 30 has not only failed to appreciate in value lately, but some models have actually lost ground. This makes them terrible investments and wonderful buys for the collector who isn't put off by magnetos, rear transmissions or right-hand drive. These are big, pleasing cars to drive, laden with brass, quite reliable once you get them right and certain to impress onlookers. A runabout at $50,000, maybe even $40,000, in good condition, is the most desirable body style.

Prices for good open 18s range around $30,000–$40,000; closed models in top condition would certainly command less, despite their greater scarcity. Brass-age Packards come up for sale rarely, so you may have to settle for what you can get, and you'll only get it by joining some clubs and placing a lot of want ads.

Despite their lower production, a few 18s have survived to join the 30s in antique auto circles—though, alas, fewer are seen in action and more are found motionless in museums or private collections. One exception, a handsome tonneau owned by Ernie Gill of Maryland, was admired on the 1977 Glidden Tour, where it ascended Pikes Peak, Colorado, with the best of its 30 hp and 40 hp siblings. The most desirable 18 is the two-seat runabout, a strong performer with its light coachwork.

While Packard catalogs cite numerous body styles for 18s and 30s, the chances of your being offered anything other than a touring model or a runabout are slim. Most closed bodies disappeared when the cars ceased being regular transportation; owners who kept them generally kept the sportier open bodies, and 90 percent of the open bodies were touring or runabout types.

By comparison to the 30 and 18, the earlier Models K, L, N and 24 are so rare as to preclude any generalities, but their prices will not exceed $40,000, except for special, well-known examples. One of these is the famous Model L touring restored by the late Dick Teague, now at the Henry Ford Museum in Dearborn, Michigan, which is certainly worth every bit of $60,000. This is largely due to its exquisite condition and its association with a famous Packard designer.

Membership in a multimake antique car club is recommended for buyers of these Packards. Many antique Packard owners consider the Packard clubs to be "postwar groups" and feel happier with cars of their same era. This is too bad, because in fact the Packard clubs devote considerably more ink to antiques than do multimake clubs. More pre–1920 Packards ought to appear at Packard club meets as their owners are missing much.

Problem Areas

Old brass is hard to find and notoriously difficult to restore once badly damaged or worn; acetylene lighting systems likewise require an expert's hand. Mechanical components of these Packards are relatively straightforward, and if a part doesn't exist it

Packard towed the mark with the Selden Patent interests. Until Henry Ford broke the hammer-lock, Selden demanded a royalty from all manufacturers, claiming to have "invented" the car. *Henry Ford Museum*

PLAN OF CHASSIS.

A strong ladder chassis with braced cross-members and right-hand drive was typical of all Packard Fours.

can generally be machined. Bodywork is simple, relative to later model Packards, and can usually be replicated; many bodies now on these early chassis were fabricated from scratch and may not be completely authentic. Finding Packard manuals and catalogs to

This Model NA, or 18, tourer represented Packard's downmarket model. The company published detailed guides to paint schemes, typically, as here, Packard Blue with Cream striping.

A 1908 Model U, or 30, tourer with victoria top displayed its greater wheelbase—compared with that of the 18—elaborate interior and plethora of brass.

Enjoying a Rhode Island tour is this couple at speed in a handsome 1907 Model U runabout, as beautiful an antique Packard as anyone is likely to encounter. *Jack Connors*

document the design of any part or body component is a major challenge. If you have any doubt about the originality of a body, an expert's advice is strongly recommended.

Identification

Model K: None are known to exist.

Model L: Ox-yoke grille and high cycle or wing fenders; aluminum body; standard paint Richelieu Blue with black molding and cream striping and running gear.

Model N: New closed body styles and side instead of rear entrance to tonneau models.

24 (Model S): Black-painted hex design in hub ends, magneto ignition and much longer wheelbase.

30 (Model U): Longer wheelbase and hood, headlights standard; much larger engine with larger, flat-top valve chambers;

The 1909 18 town landaulet, a popular semi-closed body style at the time. None are known to exist now.

bayonet radiator cap in 1908; mudguard fenders, cellular radiator and reserve fuel tank in 1909; dry plate instead of expanding ring clutch, larger and deeper fenders and larger steering wheel in 1910; new Packard Blue paint scheme with grey running gear and black striping in 1911; clutch remounted behind engine, standard oil-and-electric side and rear lights with acetylene headlamps standard in 1912.

18 (Model NA): 266 ci T-head engine and shorter wheelbases than comparable 30s. Sliding gear rear transmission in 1909; changes that paralleled the 30 for 1910-1912.

Production

Model	1907	1908	1909	1910	1911	1912	Total
K	—	—	—	—	—	—	34 (1903)
L	—	—	—	—	—	—	207 (1904)
N	—	—	—	—	—	—	403 (1905)
24 (S)	—	—	—	—	—	—	728 (1906)
30 (U)	1,128	1,303	1,501	2,493	1,865	1,250	9,540
18 (NA)	—	—	802	766	360	350	2,278

Specifications

Model	Cyl	Bore x Stroke	CI	Bhp	Wheelbase
K	4	4.00 x 5.00 in.	315	24	92 in.
L	4	3.88 x 5.13	242	22	94
N	4	4.06 x 5.13	262	28	106
24 (S)	4	4.50 x 5.50	350	24	108, 119
30 (U)	4	5.00 x 5.50	432	30	108, 122, 123, 129.5
18 (NA)	4	4.06 x 5.13	262	18	102, 108, 112

Chassis and drivetrain: Ladder chassis with semi-elliptic leaf springs front and rear, rear clutch and transmission; bevel gear differential on Models N, 24, 30 and 18; shock absorbers standard on 1910-1912 30 and 18. Curb weight 2,500 to 5,000 lb.

Bodies:

1903 Model K: Tonneau.

1904 Model L: Runabout, surrey, tonneau.

1905 Model N: Brougham, limousine, runabout, tonneau, touring.

1906 24 (Model S): Landaulet, limousine, runabout, touring, victoria.

1907-1912 30 (Model U): Landaulet, limousine, runabout, touring; close-coupled touring in 1908-1909; brougham; coupe in 1911-1912; demi-limousine in 1909-1910; Imperial landaulet and limousine in 1912; phaeton in 1910-1912; town car in 1910-1911.

1909-1912 18 (Model NA): Landaulet, limousine, runabout, touring; close-coupled touring in 1911; coupe in 1911-1912; demi-limousine in 1909; Imperial landaulet and limousine in 1912.

Motor Numbers

Model L: 501-705

Model N: 1002-1405

24 (Model S): 2003-2729

30 (Model U): 5006-6311 in 1907-1908, 6481-7086 and 7501-8999 in 1909, 10000-11999 and 13001-13518 in 1910, 15001-15999 and 16000-16884 in 1911, 20001-23000 in 1912

18 (Model NA): 9001-9801 in 1909, 12001-12837 in 1910, 18801-19176 in 1911, 26001-27000 in 1912

Price History

95+ point condition 1	1982	1987	1992	Return
18 Open	$40,000	$42,000	$45,000	2.4%
30 Open	65,000	60,000	55,000	-3.4
18 Closed	20,000	22,500	25,000	4.5
30 Closed	30,000	32,500	35,000	3.1

Chapter 3

Sixes, 1912–1915

Models 48 and 38

	Fun	Investment	Anguish
48 Open	10	6	8
48 Closed	6	4	8
38 Open	9	6	8
38 Closed	6	4	8

The big Six of 1912–1915 was the grandest Packard of them all. Despite some important cars before it, and many distinguished ones still to come, no other Packard was as large or was built with as much painstaking hand labor, and none would ever duplicate the slow-turning, lazily powerful engine. A runabout for two passengers on a 144 in. wheelbase was strictly a Six phenomenon, unmatched by any other Packard before or after.

The culmination of Henry Joy's decade of management, the Six was, as Joy was quoted in contemporary Packard ads, "graceful of line, impeccable in finish, silent in action, powerful and swift." Technically, it was a significant car that spanned the transition from oil to electric lighting, right-hand to left-hand drive, T-head to L-head engines. Sixes also introduced the modern idea of grouping all controls on a panel within easy reach of the driver's hand.

Yet the Six lasted only four years before it was replaced by "a modern formula," the Twin Six—a fine car in its own right, but without that let-them-eat-cake brand of luxury that the Six had offered.

What Packard called the Dominant Six would accelerate 0–60 mph in 30 sec. in 1912—astonishing for a production car. In 1915, a 48 hp Six averaged 70 mph on twenty-nine laps of the Indianapolis Speed-

way, while a smaller 38 hp model did twenty-six laps at more than 60 mph. Three quarters of a century later these were not even legal speeds in some states; in 1915 it seemed, as research engineer W. R. McCulla said at the time, "nothing short of a miracle."

Packard had planned to call the first 1912 Six the 36 after its Association of Licensed

The only complete closed-model 48 is this magnificent limousine owned by Ed Marion of Florida, familiar to many from its long tour and meet career.

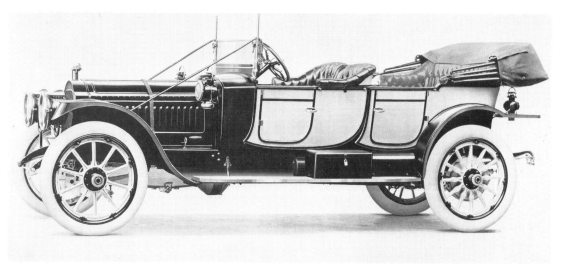

The 1912 Six, the first six-cylinder Packard, shared its body styling, gas headlamps and right-hand drive with the 30 and 18, which were concurrent models that year.

Auto Manufacturers (ALAM) horsepower rating. But that figure turned out to be 48, and the model was named accordingly. Even this figure was misleading, since the 525 ci T-head engine put out about 72 bhp. The engine rode a sturdy ladder chassis with a 56.5 in. track, had a standard 139 in. wheelbase (shorter for runabouts) and was vastly better proportioned than, though similar in design to, the 30 and 18, which shared the

The original 48 engine was cast in three blocks of two cylinders; beginning with the 1914 4-48, it was two blocks of three and was rotated 180 degrees to allow left-hand drive.

line one final year in 1912. The 30 and 18 were soon dropped; Packard sold only 282 of them against 1,349 of the 1912 Six.

The smaller 38 model, introduced in 1913 and likewise named for its ALAM rating, was hardly less heroically proportioned than the 48, but its L-head engine was new and displaced fewer cubic inches. The 38 bristled with innovations: a seven-main-bearing crankshaft against only four mains in the 48; Packard's first self-starter; left-hand drive; and the remarkable central control panel with lighting, starting, carburetion and ignition controls all within easy reach, a precursor of the modern dashboard.

"The temptation arises from time to time to make vehicles of cheaper character," said Henry Joy, "but the conclusion is always reached that such a change in policy would not give 'Packard' results. . . . We have just one way of doing things. We are going to keep right on along the same lines as long as we stay in business."

Series Nomenclature

The Packard Six was the first model in which Packard adopted series rather than model year identification. This has caused a good deal of confusion among collectors, which we will now proceed to unravel. Follow carefully—it's very confusing!

The initial model—the 1912 Six (48 hp)—was designated by model year in the conventional manner.

In early 1913, Packard was still using model year terminology: 1348 for the 1913 48 hp model, 1338 for the newly announced 38 hp model.

On March 1, 1913, Packard considered that the year was far enough along to re-designate the 38 a 1914 model so the 1338 became the 1438, with no change in specification. The 1348 had meanwhile ceased production. The company built its two Sixes alternately, not simultaneously, and this was the reason for the eventual use of series nomenclature.

Later in 1913, 38 production stopped and Packard began building the 48 again, a T-head model with right-hand drive similar to the 1348. This car was again named for its model year: 1448. It was the last in which

Packard would retain a model year designation.

Early in 1914, the 48 was completely changed, adopting an L-head engine, left-hand drive and other characteristics pioneered by the 38. It was too soon to call this new 48 a 1915 model, but its predecessor had already carried the designation 1448.

What to do? The answer was series nomenclature. This new L-head, left-hand drive 48 became known as the 4-48 or Fourth Series 48. For uniformity, Packard later referred to the 1912 Six as the 1-48, the 1913 1348 as 2-48, and the early 1914 1448 as 3-48.

The fifth and final 48 saw little change and coincided neatly with the model year, but Packard retained series nomenclature, dubbing it the 5-48.

On 38 hp Packards, series nomenclature developed similarly. In 1914, a revised 38 replaced the original model; Packard thought it too early to call this a 1915 model or 1538, so they designated it by series: 2-38. The third and final 38, sold during the 1915 model year, was thus the 3-38.

Packard would use series nomenclature for the rest of its history. In the late 1930s it became superfluous, because changes coincided strictly with model years. Nevertheless, it is correct to refer to a 1953 Patrician

Atop Pikes Peak on the 1977 Glidden Tour, with Don Weber, left, and crew and Weber's 1914 Model 1448 (3-48). The Six made the ascent without even breathing hard.

The most desirable Six body style, but unfortunately rare, is the phaeton-runabout, this one a Model 1438 photographed in the Packard studios in July 1913. Notable changes introduced by the 38 were the control panel under the steering wheel, left-hand drive and electric lights.

as a "Twenty-sixth Series." (In 1954 the series was aligned to the model year and the 1954 Patrician became part of the Fifty-fourth Series. The last Packards ever built, in 1958, were thus the Fifty-eighth Series.)

What To Look For

Only two dozen 48s and about as many 38s are known to exist, including parts cars and chassis. We are therefore talking about extremely rare cars, and you will have few

This sensational "victoria park carriage" was custom-built by Brewster for Mrs. E.H.G. Slater of Washington, DC, on a 38 chassis. Finding it would be a coup.

choices if you want one. Packard Sixes are usually exchanged quietly between friends; their owners know each other and communicate regularly.

The Packard Club maintains a register of all known cars, and the registrar, Don Weber, should be consulted for information on any for sale. Weber's former 1914 Model 1448 was a well-known car on the Glidden and other antique car tours. Equally knowledgeable and experienced in restoration is Phil Hill of Hill & Vaughn Restorations in Santa Monica, California.

Most 48s and 38s are touring, phaeton or runabout models; the only complete closed car known to exist is a 1914 Model 1448 limousine in Florida. Although engines and drivetrains differed between 38 and 48, bodies were completely interchangeable, and dealers and owners switched them regularly. So it is quite appropriate to have, say, a 5-48 chassis with a body bearing 3-38 serial numbers. This is in fact the case with the two 5-48s known to exist, both located in California and one owned by Phil Hill.

More important is this question: Is the body an original Packard body, restored in part, or completely fabricated? The latter should be examined carefully with reference to original photos and Packard publications for correctness in every detail.

Identification

The 48s: 1912 Six or 1-48: The First Series 48. Right-hand drive, T-head engine, gas headlights, oil sidelights.

1913 1348 or 2-48: The Second Series 48. Right-hand drive, T-head engine, electric headlights and combination oil-electric sidelights.

1914 1448 or 3-48: The Third Series 48. Left-hand drive, T-head engine, electric headlights, combination oil-electric sidelights, combination electric starter-generator and control board under steering wheel.

1914 4-48: The Fourth Series 48. Left-hand drive, L-head engine, all-electric lights, starter and control board.

1915 5-48: The Fifth Series 48. As above, with auxiliary lights in same housing with headlamps and combination rear lamp and license light.

The 38s: 1913 1338 or 1-38: The First Series 38. Left-hand drive with electric headlamps and control board on all models. Engine cast in three blocks of two, oil-electric sidelights and electric starter-generator.

1914 1438 or 1-38: Continuation of the First Series 38, identical to the 1338 except for model year. Packard changed from 1338 to 1438 on March 1, 1913, at which point only 678 1338s (through serial number 38678) had been built. The remaining 980 were therefore called 1438s.

1914 2-38: The Second Series 38, with engine cast in two blocks of three cylinders each and separate electric starter.

1915 3-38: The Third Series 38, identical to the 2-38 except for combination headlight-auxiliary light taillight-license light.

Motor Numbers
The 48s
1912 Six (1-48): 23001-26000
1913 2-48: 35026-37999
1914 1448 (3-48): 50026-52000
1914 4-48: 63026-66000
1915 5-48: 78026-78586
The 38s
1913 1338 (1-38): 38000-38678
1914 1438 (1-38): 38679-42000
1914 2-38: 53026-56000
1915 3-38: 75026-76999

Production

Model	1912	1913	Early 1914	Late 1914[1]	1915
48	1,349	1,000	1,499[2]	441[3]	360
38	—	678	980[4]	1,501[5]	1,801

Footnotes:

[1]Two different types of both 48 and 38 were produced in the 1914 model year.

[2]The 1448 or 3-48, with right-hand drive and T-head engine.

[3]The 4-48, with left-hand drive and L-head engine.

[4]The 1438 (identical to 1338, both models considered the First Series 38 or 1-38), with

engine cast in three blocks of two cylinders each, combination oil-electric sidelights and electric starter-generator.

Specifications

Model	Head	Bore x Stroke	CI	Bhp	Wheelbase
1–48	T	4.50 x 5.50 in.	525	74	121.5, 133, 139 in.
2–48	T	4.50 x 5.50	525	82	121.5, 133, 139
3–48	T	4.50 x 5.50	525	82	121.5, 139
4–48	L	4.50 x 5.50	525	82	121.5, 139, 144
5–48	L	4.50 x 5.50	525	82	121.5, 139, 144
1–38	L	4.00 x 5.50	415	60	115.5, 134
2–38	L	4.00 x 5.50	415	60	115.5, 134, 140
3–38	L	4.00 x 5.50	415	65	115.5, 134, 140

[5]The Second Series 1914 38 or 2–38, with engine cast in two blocks of three cylinders each and separate electric starter.

Chassis and drivetrain: Ladder chassis with semi-elliptic springs; three-quarter elliptic rear springs (2–48 to 5–48 and all 38s); rear-mounted sliding gear transmission, spiral bevel gears on 1914–1915 models. Curb weight from 3,100 lb. on 1–38 runabout to 5,200 lb. on 5–48 limousine.

Bodies:

Available on all models included brougham, coupe, Imperial limousine, phaeton, runabout and touring.

Bodies available on various models included for the 1912 Six: Canopy touring, close-coupled touring, Imperial landaulet, landaulet, limousine, victoria phaeton, victoria touring.

1914 3–48: Cabette, Imperial coupe, landaulet, limousine, phaeton-runabout, salon brougham, victoria touring.

1914 4–48: Cab-sides landaulet, cab-sides limousine, Imperial coupe, landaulet, limousine.

1915 5–48: Landaulet, limousine, salon brougham, salon limousine.

1913–1914 1–38: Close-coupled touring, Imperial coupe, Imperial landaulet, landaulet, limousine, victoria phaeton, victoria touring.

1914 2–38: All-weather convertible, cab-sides limousine, close-coupled touring, limousine, salon brougham, salon limousine, salon touring, special touring.

1915 3–38: All-weather convertible, cab-sides landaulet, cab-sides limousine, Imperial coupe, landaulet, limousine, salon brougham, salon limousine, salon touring, special touring.

Price History

95+ point condition 1	1982	1987	1992	Return
48 Open	$75,000	$90,000	$100,000	6.0%
38 Open	57,500	70,000	85,000	8.1

Note: Old-car price guides that fill in prices for every model produced are unrealistic. Aside from a single limousine, *no* closed-body Sixes are known to exist. Remember that bodies for these cars were easily interchangeable; most owners had a closed body for winter and an open one for summer. Since closed bodies, containing more wood and cloth, deteriorated faster and were discarded earlier, the open bodies survived. A newly discovered Model 48 salon brougham or limousine would be an important find and would cost as much as an open model.

Among extant open cars, the pecking order is thus: runabout, phaeton and touring. A surviving example of the exquisite 1914 Model 4–48 runabout, on its majestic wheelbase of 144 in., has never turned up; if found, it would probably be worth $200,000.

Chapter 4

Twin Six, 1916–1923

Models 25 and 35

	Fun	Investment	Anguish
Open models	8	5	8
Closed models	5	3	8

The Twin Six, conceived by Packard's brilliant chief engineer Jesse Vincent, was rushed into production more to confound the competition than to improve on the Six. The luxury car field was moving toward eight- and twelve-cylinder power, and Cadillac had introduced its revolutionary V–8 in 1915. Packard's first Twelve was a realistic response. Moreover, the Twin was favorably received, and with Packard's continuing expansion into export markets, it was the car that established the company's worldwide reputation. Throughout the era of the Twin Six, advertisements were able to claim that more Packards were touring abroad each summer than any other make of American car and sometimes the Packards outnumbered all other American makes put together. The reason was that the Twins were powerful and reliable, and Packard had established a strong overseas dealer network.

Packard had gone from model year to series nomenclature during the Six era (for a thorough explanation of how this occurred, please refer to the previous chapter). Series nomenclature was retained during the eight years of Twin Six production and there were three distinct series. Most changes occurred early. Thus the First Series Twin Six corresponded to model year 1916, the Second Series to 1917, and the Third Series to the model years 1918–1923.

The Twin continued evolving toward modern concepts, moving the transmission from the rear axle to aft of the clutch and offering a wide variety of closed as well as open bodies. Prices were reduced from those of the Six, resulting in a sales spurt: Production in 1916 alone almost equaled the total output of Sixes. By 1923, when the Twin Six was finally retired, Packard had produced more than 35,000.

The mighty Twin Six powerplant, perfectly restored on Davis Phinney's 1919 Twin Six from Connecticut, is accurate down even to the Packard spark plugs.

Many Twin Sixes today are not accurate restorations; this 1916 example carries a bumper from the mid-1920s, probably from a Packard Eight. Careful research is essential. *Rick Lenz*

The First Series, model year 1916, comprised two models, the 1–25 and 1–35, on wheelbases of 125 and 135 in. respectively. On the Second Series 2–25 and 2–35 for 1917, Packard lengthened the shorter wheelbase by 1.5 in., fitted detachable cylinder heads and a removable thermostat. Smaller wheels and more streamlined bodies made the 1917 models much lower in stance.

The Third Series 3–25 and 3–35 had more horsepower through a revised head design, better breathing and slightly longer wheelbases. After the end of the First World War, the 3–25 was dropped, but the 3–35 soldiered on into 1923. The most notable development during this period was the Fuelizer, a manifold-mounted spark plug designed to help vaporize the fuel-air mixture, which arrived in 1919.

What To Look For

Like the Sixes, most surviving Twin Sixes are open, the seven-passenger touring being the most common body style. However, more cars are available to choose from. Situated in the borderland between pre-1915 horseless carriages and 1925–1948 Classics, the Twin Six demonstrates neither the flat appreciation curve of most antiques nor the upward spiraling prices of most Classics. Good restorations enjoy strong, steady, but

On tour near the Grand Tetons, a Second Series 1917 Twin Six owned by Howard Henry of Maryland. The distance driven suggests the Twin Six's continued reliability today.

not spectacular growth in value. The rare closed models have appreciated faster than the typical certificate of deposit. In terms of investment, the most notable models are open Twins bearing special or custom bodies by such makers as Fleetwood, which supplied some Packard owners in the years before it became part of General Motors.

Few restorations are being performed on Twin Sixes today; most examples were restored years ago and show varying degrees of wear and tear. Serious, body-off restoration may nevertheless be contemplated because the expertise exists—and any major work should include body removal, which is not hard because it was often done annually when the cars were current.

Early restorers cut a lot of corners, so bodies should be examined for alterations to the original design. Expert help is essential. No Twin Six service instructions or overhaul manuals are available, and few copies of the parts list exist.

Lacking printed documentation, the serious restorer should examine authentic cars for comparison. Fine Twin Sixes are held by the Frederick Crawford Museum in Cleveland and the Henry Ford Museum in Dearborn. Among several collectors with long Twin Six experience I recommend Bradley Skinner and Davis G. Phinney (see the Parts and Services section at the end of this book).

In 1978, Phinney wrote a definitive restoration article on his 1919 Third Series Twin

Davis Phinney's award-winning 1919 Twin Six touring was restored in a massive effort involving scores of people and meticulous research. It is probably the best in the world.

Details of the Phinney Twin Six show the
instrumentation.

The Motometer with Packard Liberty aircraft
engine logo.

Hard-to-find Packard spark plugs—components of the perfect restoration.

Six touring, with detailed drawings and documentation, in *The Packard Cormorant*, number 10.

Problem Areas

Like all antique Packards, finding the right parts is the most-cited problem area. Like the Six and its predecessors, many engine components can be machined if necessary, but the Twin Six was a more complicated machine and the process involves time and money. Determining authenticity of a Twin Six body is another problem area; here, buyers should take advice from one of the acknowledged Twin Six experts. Happily, a lot more Twin Sixes exist than earlier Packard models, so there is an ample supply for comparison purposes.

Production

Model	1916	1917	1918–1919	1920–1923
25	3,606	4,950	4,181	—
35	4,140	4,049	5,406	8,770

A Third Series Twin Six from circa 1920, photographed in front of the East Grand Boulevard factory. This was a custom body, possibly by Fleetwood, with dual cowl and landau top. Drum headlights and disc wheels were popular in the early 1920s.

Identification

1916 First Series: High-built bodies with 36 in. wheels front and 37 in. wheels rear; 125 in. and 135 in. wheelbases.

1917 Second Series: Lower bodies with 35 in. wheels all around; 126.5 in. and 135 in. wheelbases.

1918–1923 Third Series: Gearshift lever relocated from left of steering column to center of floor; 128 in. and 136 in. wheelbases. The presence of a Fuelizer does not necessarily denote a post–1919 model, since some were retrofitted to earlier cars.

Motor Numbers

1916 First Series: 80000–87787
1917 Second Series: 125051–15000
1918–1919 Third Series: 150051–up
1920–1923 Third Series: 21000–22300

Specifications

Year	Type	Bore x Stroke	CI	Bhp	Wheelbase
1916	V–12	3.00 x 5.00 in.	424	88	125, 135 in.
1917	V–12	3.00 x 5.00	424	88	126.5, 135
1918–1923	V–12	3.00 x 5.00	424	90	128, 136

Chassis and drivetrain: Ladder chassis; solid axles with semi-elliptic leaf springs; wire or artillery wheels; live rear axle with spiral bevel gears, three-speed sliding gear transmission. Curb weight from 4,150 lb. for runabout to 4,970 lb. for Imperial limousine.

Bodies:

1916–1919 Model 35: Brougham, cab-sides limousine, Imperial limousine, landaulet, limousine, phaeton, salon phaeton, salon touring.

1916–1919 Model 25: Brougham, coupe, landaulet, limousine, phaeton, runabout (25 only), salon phaeton, salon touring.

1920–1923 Model 35: Coupe, duplex coupe, duplex sedan, limousine, phaeton, runabout, touring.

Price History

95+ point condition 1	1982	1987	1992	Return
Open	$35,000	$40,000	$45,000	5.2%
Closed	20,000	29,000	38,000	13.7

Chapter 5

Single Six and Six, 1920–1928

Models 116, 226, 233, 326, 333, 426, 433, 526 and 533

	Fun	Investment	Anguish
1921–1924 Closed	3	3	6
1921–1924 Open	6	5	6
1925–1928 Closed	4	7	6
1925–1928 Open	7	8	6

Packard's first period of economic doldrums occurred during the post World War I recession, when the number of buyers capable of writing $7,000 checks thinned appreciably.

Buying on time did not exist, and if it had, Packard dealers would probably have considered it beneath them. Packard's response—and a sound one it was—came in 1921: the

Spare and angular, the original Model 116 Single Six was not a glamorous looker, but it saved Packard's bacon during the recession of the early 1920s. *Eastern Packard Club*

Less severe with its polished radiator, this 1923 Six was owned by Sir Hubert Herkomer, founder of Britain's Herkomer Trials, Hertfordshire, England. *National Motor Museum*

Single Six, a boxy affair with closed bodies by Pullman on a short wheelbase, with an L-head six-cylinder engine that had nothing in common with the great Sixes of 1912–

1915. For a fine account of the corporate decision making that resulted in the Single Six, see "Saga of the 116," by C. A. Leslie, Jr., in *The Packard Cormorant*, number 34.

As it had since 1914, Packard designated the Single Six by series. The boxy original was the First Series Model 116; its longer, lower successors for 1922–1923 were the 226 and 233. By 1928, the final year of the Six, it had reached its Fifth Series with the Models 526 and 533. This was the beginning of the series designations that Packard maintained right on up through 1953. For a complete rundown of all models, see the Identification section further in this chapter.

The Single Six was first offered in only four basic body styles at prices starting around $2,500, and no doubt it brought a needed infusion of cash into Packard's coffers. Sales were sluggish for the first two years but took off with a snap in 1922–1923, when more than 18,000 Single Sixes were sold—about 80 percent of Packard's total production, including trucks.

Some Singles were custom-bodied by foreign coachbuilders, as was this handsome salon by Grosvenor of London on a 1924 chassis. Wheel covers are also custom. *National Motor Museum*

A Single Six chassis is laid out in typical orderly progression. *Detroit Public Library*

For 1925, Packard renamed the car the Six, added several new bodies including a phaeton and club sedan, and broadened the color choices, also raising the price somewhat. The Packard Six now looked much like the Packard Eight, and sales of nearly 25,000 of the 1925–1926 Model 326 were the highest for any individual Packard model in history. Over eight years the Six racked up more than 154,000 sales, which was the best

This superb maroon Single Six runabout was long owned by Bev Ferreira of San Francisco. By 1925, the Six had become much like the Packard Eight, with more rounded, attractive lines. *Bud Juneau*

total Packard had ever experienced to date for any model.

Why then did Packard drop the Six after 1928? Competitive pressure and the rapidly recovering car market of the late 1920s seem to be the reasons. Packard's standard Eight in 1929 was the successor to the Six, deliberately styled to look like it; Packard firmly opposed dynamic obsolescence. The standard Eight was intended to stem the rush of upper-medium-priced-car buyers into competitors like Cadillac's new LaSalle, which was also an eight.

Dropping the Six proved to be a mistake, because the market would collapse in the early 1930s as quickly as it had expanded in the late 1920s, following the stock market crash and the subsequent Depression. But nobody knew this then.

What To Look For

When it was founded, the Classic Car Club of America arbitrarily set 1925 as the beginning of the Classic era, which resulted in striking inconsistencies, and the Packard Six is the most commonly cited example. Packardians complain that the 1924 Six is virtually the same as the 1925, but the 1925 is a Classic and the 1924 is not. One supposes the CCCA had to start somewhere; 1925 is a logical beginning for what we commonly consider the golden age of the automobile. Nevertheless, the organization's decision affects values. There is a definite

A Fifth Series Six, probably a Model 533 phaeton. Note the restrained color scheme and blackwall tires—not popular today among collectors, who often tend to overcolor and over-equip such cars.

price gap between non-Classic pre-1925 Packard Sixes and 1925–1928 models. The 1928s, with their sleek new phaeton and two-passenger runabout bodies, are the most desirable of all. The most you can or should pay for a Six at this writing is about $60,000, for a show-stopping 1928 phaeton or runabout.

If you're not bothered about Classic status, pre-1925 open Sixes are good buys, running just more than $30,000 in 1992 for the best ninety-point open examples. Good closed models of these early Single Sixes could be had for $20,000, whereas closed 1925–1928 Classics run $10,000 higher. The most rapid appreciators in the 1980s were the 1925–1927 closed models.

Problem Areas

The Single Six and Six engines were simple and reliable, but require due care and attention, considering that they are more than sixty years old. Old-style water pumps use special packing and require periodic tightening. Brakes need frequent adjustment, which is no fun, and even when adjusted they don't perform as well as modern equipment. Vacuum-tank fuel systems of the 1920s can give frequent annoyance and may run out of gas on a long climb. Engine water jackets rust out and require replacement. These were just the normal trials of motoring in the 1920s and should be expected.

One other problem area involves the wood that frames the bodies. If it has rotted significantly, major and expensive repairs await. On affected cars, the doors will not hang properly and the whole car will shake. Check all wood carefully.

Serial Numbers
1920–1922 Model 116: 26–8850
1922–1923 Models 126 and 133: 9000–35942
1924 Models 226 and 233: 37000–48917
1925–1926 Models 326 and 333: 49501–90463
1927 Models 426 and 433: 95007–120407
1928 Models 526 and 533: 125013–166770

Identification
1920–1922 Model 116: Upright, truncated body on 116 in. wheelbase only; fixed quarter lights ahead of doors.

1922–1923 Models 126 and 133: Longer, lower body styling; nine-plate clutch; more horsepower; water pump moved to front of engine; broad expansion of body styles; 126 in. and 133 in. wheelbases, respectively.

1924 Models 226 and 233: Four-wheel brakes; horizontally divided windshield with single wiper. Last model called Single Six.

1925–1926 Models 326 and 333: Renamed Six; disc wheels standard, Bijur lubrication system and new body styles including club sedan and Holbrook coupe.

1927 Models 426 and 433: Phenomenal 33 percent increase in brake horsepower, no Fuelizer, hypoid rear axle.

1928 Models 526 and 533: Oil filter standard, four-point instead of three-point engine mounting, cowl lights optional and first offering of coachbuilt body styles on Six.

Production

Model	1920–1922	1922–1923	1924	1925–1926	1927	1928
116	8,800	—	—	—	—	—
126–526	—	18,192	8,094	24,668	14,401	28,336
133–533	—	8,368	3,131	15,690	10,934	13,414

Specifications

Year	Model	Bore x Stroke	CI	Bhp	Wheelbase
1920–1922	116	3.38 x 4.50 in.	241.5	52	116 in.
1922–1923	126, 133	3.38 x 4.50	241.5	54	126, 133
1924	226, 233	3.38 x 5.00	268.4	54	126, 133
1925–1926	326, 333	3.50 x 5.00	288.6	60	126, 133
1927	426, 433	3.50 x 5.00	288.6	81	126, 133
1928	526, 533	3.50 x 5.00	288.6	81	126, 133

Chassis and drivetrain: Ladder chassis, beam axles, torsion tubes and semi-elliptic springs front and rear, rear brakes only, four-wheel brakes introduced on 226 and 233, Bijur lubrication introduced on 326 and 333. Curb weight from 2,790 lb. on 116 runabout to 4,205 lb. on 533 sedan-limousine.

Bodies:

1920–1922 Model 116: Touring, runabout, sedan, coupe.

1922–1924 Models 126 and 226: Coupe (various passenger capacities), runabout, sedan, sedan-limousine, sport, touring, touring sedan.

1925–1926 Model 326: Same as 226 plus phaeton.

1927 Model 426: Phaeton, roadster, sedan.

1928 Model 526: Convertible coupe, coupe, phaeton, runabout, sedan.

1922–1924 Models 133 and 233: Limousine, long-wheelbase sedan, touring.

1925–1926 Model 333: Same as 233 plus club sedan.

1927 Model 433: Coupe, club sedan, sedan, sedan-limousine.

1928 Model 533: Same as 433 plus phaeton, runabout, touring.

Price History

95+ point condition 1	1982	1987	1992	Return
1920–1924 Open	$18,000	$23,000	$32,000	12.2%
1920–1924 Closed	12,000	18,000	25,000	15.8
1925–1927 Open	16,000	28,000	38,000	18.9
1925–1927 Closed	10,000	20,000	32,000	26.2
1928 Open	30,000	45,000	55,000	12.9
1928 Closed	19,000	24,000	30,000	9.6

Chapter 6

Eights, 1924–1931

Models 136, 143, 236, 243, 336, 343, 443, 626, 633, 640, 645, 726, 733, 740, 745, 826, 833, 840 and 845

	Fun	Investment	Anguish
Open	8	8	5
Closed	4	5	5

Packard's success in the Classic era was built upon these cars. Though eclipsed by such novelties as the individual customs and Speedster Eights of 1929 and beyond, and the Twelve after 1932, Packard's "standard"

Eight remained its breadwinner. Until 1929 it was outsold by the Packard Six, but once the Six disappeared and the Eight expanded down-market, it became Packard's most important model. As the Depression deepened

Dramatically beautiful were the custom-bodied Eights by Dietrich, this example being a two- passenger coupe. Note dual spares and, again, the conservative paint scheme and black tires.

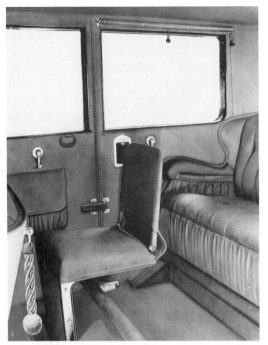

Broadcloth upholstery and woolen carpets decorate the interior of an early Eight limousine, complete with privacy shades for rear windows and elaborate assist pulls.

in 1931, the standard Eight was all that stood between Packard and bankruptcy. More than 15,000 were sold in 1931, which was not much by 1929 standards but enough to keep Packard going—a sales figure that Pierce, for example, would have welcomed.

Through 1931, these Eights were offered in seven series numbered First through Eighth but skipping Fifth, which was confined to the Six. From 1924–1928, the model designation represented the series and wheelbase. For example, a 443 is a 1928 Fourth Series on the 143 in. wheelbase.

During 1929–1931 on the Sixth through Eighth Series, the model designation was approximately, but not exactly, in line with the wheelbase. In each of these years there were four models. In 1930, for example, these were the 726, 733, 740 and 745, but the wheelbase of the 726 was 127.5 in. For detailed discussions of these various models, refer to the Identification and Specifications sections which follow.

Arriving complete with four-wheel brakes and a dramatically longer hood than the Single Six, the 1924 First Series Single Eight was structured along Six lines aft of the cowl

This 1929 Eight roadster is owned by the Henry Ford Museum. *Henry Ford Museum*

but finished in more elegant materials. Starting around $3,700, about $1,000 more than the Single Six, the Single Eight was equipped with Fuelizer, Watson Stabilizer shock absorbers, Motometer radiator cap (registering water temperature for the driver), disc wheels, bumpers front and rear, a tire pump operating off the gearbox, and a four-point-mounted Eight with nine main bearings and a vibration damper.

The 1925 Second Series was known simply as the Packard Eight, adding Bijur automatic chassis lubrication, controlled by a button on the dashboard. In early 1926, still on the Second Series, Packard introduced a handsome variety of factory custom bodies by coachbuilders Derham, Dietrich, Fleetwood, Holbrook and Judkins on the longer, 143 in. wheelbase.

Having attended to the body department, Packard made drivetrain improvements to the 1927 Third Series. It had a larger engine with the manifold and combustion chamber redesigned for more power, aluminum pistons, a new two-plate instead of multi-disc clutch and a hypoid rear axle. The Holbrook coupe, previously a standard factory offering, was a custom body, along with a new custom phaeton.

Attempting to outflank the competition at both ends of its market, Packard dramatically upgraded the 1928 Fourth Series Eights with a single long-wheelbase chassis and a posh line of Custom Eights, while cutting prices for standard Eights. Packard now offered nine Eights with starting prices under $4,000, which caused a major surge in sales. Not all Custom Eights were genuine customs; the bodies matched those of the standard Eight. However, Packard had expanded the range of custom bodies enormously, cataloging a score of designs from the five coachbuilders mentioned above plus LeBaron, Murphy and Rollston.

The 1929 Eights were designated the Sixth Series, skipping the Fifth, so as not to be confused with the Fifth Series Sixes, which had ceased production in 1928. To take the place of the Six, Packard offered a standard Eight with a new, smaller engine. This was a year of important design and engineering changes throughout the Eight line: rounded instead of drum-type headlamps, dashboard temperature gauges instead of Motometers, Packard instead of

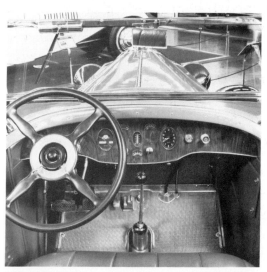

The 1929 Eight roadster. I am not sure about the material used for the dashboard. *Henry Ford Museum*

The Packard Deluxe Ornament or Goddess of Speed was a $10 accessory; the coat of arms was first used in 1928. *Henry Ford Museum*

Watson Stabilizer shock absorbers, plated instead of painted headlights. Custom and Deluxe Eights rode longer-wheelbase chassis and the new Speedster Eight was introduced (see Chapter 7).

Evolutionary changes attended the 1930 Seventh Series, including thermostatically controlled radiator shutters replacing the internal thermostat, a four-speed gearbox and Detroit Lubricator updraft carburetor. All but one standard Eight body were mounted on the longer, 134.5 in. wheelbase. The Custom and Deluxe Eights continued, but with fewer cataloged designs from only four coachbuilders: Brewster, Dietrich, LeBaron and Rollston. Individual customs were available on the Eight chassis.

Horsepower for the Eight hit 100 on the 1931 Eighth Series, and vacuum lubrication replaced the Bijur system. Fighting a depressed market, Packard expanded the number of individual custom bodies to nine on the Model 833 Eight that year—the same as the number of longer-wheelbase models— but orders were few. All long-wheelbase models were called Deluxe Eights. Significantly, of the nine individual customs offered, seven were built by Packard—the end of a long quest by management to relegate most of the custom business to Packard's own shops. The other two were by Dietrich.

What To Look For

For the past several years the 1925–1931 Packard Eight has been one of the faster-appreciating Classic cars. I place an arbitrary figure of $300,000 as the high value in 1992 of prime open custom—sport phaetons or runabouts—but it is likely that this figure has already been exceeded, either privately or at the occasional auction. This also means you can confidently dump $100,000 into the restoration of an open Eight in rough-but-complete condition and still not be overextended. One such example, at the Hershey, Pennsylvania, fall swap meet in 1989, could have been acquired for around $80,000.

The Price History section succinctly sums up desirability ratings. The non-Classic 1924 models are well down compared with the post–1924s and are consequently best buys for Packard enthusiasts who don't worry about CCCA admission. The Classics are all strong, but the closed models have generally appreciated at rates higher than those of the open models, especially individual customs. A closed car also has the advantage that chances are, it's still the original body. Replication of open bodies has been going on for years in Classic Packard circles, and some of the replicas are so good that experts are hard pressed to distinguish them from factory work.

The question sometime arises as to just how much replication is permissible or desirable. If you replace, say, a rotten wood body structure, or heavy front-end damage, with parts wholly or largely remanufactured, do you have what the antique furniture people call a married piece? This ques-

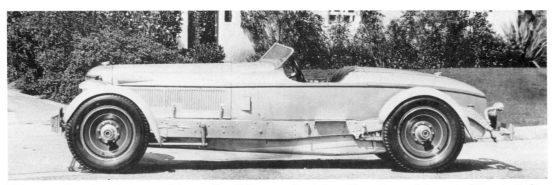

This sensational custom speedster on the 1929 Eight chassis was built for H.J.R. Glascock and featured in *The Packard Magazine* in that year.

Sculptured hood is reminiscent of Vauxhall. Car is not known to exist. *Detroit Public Library*

tion has no hard and fast answer, but most Packard people say they don't believe fabricating a fender renders a car unoriginal. On the other hand, tearing off a closed body to install an open body, even if the open body is a Packard original, raises more contention.

Problem Areas

The engines that accounted for the major portion of Classic Packard Eight production differed little in form and complexity: one was just a larger or smaller version of the other. These engines, together with the rest of the cars they powered, are stone-simple mechanically and far more reliable than contemporary automobile powerplants. The mechanical components of the cars seem to put up with anything, and even when something makes slightly more than the normal amount of noise, it is likely to keep working regardless.

Bijur and vacuum chassis lubrication systems work well, and carburetor adjustments are easy, although carburetors and associated parts are increasingly scarce.

Body troubles, aside from parts scarcity, largely involve the wood framework. Frame problems can often be detected from the sloppy fit of doors.

Production

1924: Model 136: 3,507; Model 143: 4,890
1925–1926: Model 236: 2,794; Model 243: 5,118
1927: Model 336: 1,245; Model 343: 3,241
1928: Model 443: 7,800
1929: Model 626: 26,070; Model 633: 17,060; Model 640: 9,801; Model 645: 2,061
1930: Model 726: 15,731; Model 733: 12,531; Model 740: 6,200; Model 745: 1,789
1931: Model 826: 6,009, Model 833: 6,096; Model 840: 2,035; Model 845: 1,310

Identification

1924 First Series: Single Six-type bodies on longer wheelbases, single bar bumpers, four-wheel brakes, Fuelizer, Motometer.

1925–1926 Second Series: Double bar bumpers, Bijur lubrication, Hotchkiss drive.

1927 Third Series: Fuelizer dropped on all models, hypoid differential, first phaeton model.

1928 Fourth Series: Offered only on 143 in. wheelbase in both standard and Custom models with identical bodies, differently trimmed.

Fifth Series: Did not involve Packard Eights.

1929 Sixth Series: Rounded-back headlamps replacing drum types, temperature gauge on dash, standard Eight on two shorter wheelbases.

1930 Seventh Series: Four-speed gearbox instead of three-speed, thermostat-type radiator shutters, dual fan belts, option of hood louvers or doors; laminated safety glass on 740 and 745, sidemounts standard on 745 and optional on others.

1931 Eighth Series: Vacuum lubrication replacing Bijur, larger hubcaps, three-spoke steering wheel replacing four-spoke.

Specifications

Year	Bore x Stroke	CI	Bhp	Wheelbase
1924–1926	3.38 x 5.00 in.	357.8	85	136, 143 in.
1927	3.50 x 5.00	384.8	109	136, 143
1928	3.50 x 5.00	384.8	109	143
1929–1930	3.50 x 5.00	384.8	106	126.5 (626)
				127.5 (726)
				133.5 (633)
				134.5 (733)
				140.5 (640, 740)
				145.5 (645, 745)
1931 standard	3.19 x 5.00	319.2	90	127.5 (826)
				134.5 (833)
1931 Deluxe	3.50 x 5.00	384.8	120	140.5 (840)
				145.5 (845)

Chassis and drivetrain: Ladder chassis, solid axles, semi-elliptic leaf springs and Watson (1924–1928) or Packard shock absorbers front and rear, four-wheel finned drum brakes, standard disc wheels (wood or wire wheels optional from 1929). Bijur lubrication (1926–1930), vacuum lubrication (1931). Weight from 3,200 lb. (1924 runabout) to 5,175 lb. (1931 845 all-weather town car landaulet).

Bodies (passenger capacity in parentheses):

1924 Model 136: Touring (5), runabout (2–4), sport (4), coupe (4 or 5), sedan (5), sedan limousine (5).

1924 Model 143: Touring (7), sedan-limousine (7), sedan (7).

1925–1926 Model 236: Same as 136 plus Holbrook coupe (4).

1925–1926 Model 243: Same as 143 plus club sedan (5).

1926: Same as 1925–1926 models plus the following Customs: Sedan cabriolet by Judkins; town cabriolets by Derham, Dietrich, and Fleetwood); limousine by Holbrook; convertible coupe and sedan by Dietrich.

1927 Model 336: Phaeton (5), runabout (2–4), sedan (5); other 136 in. wheelbase bodies dropped; Holbrook coupe now a custom.

1927 Model 343: Coupe (4), sedan (7), sedan limousine (7), touring (7).

1928 standard and Custom Eights: Phaeton (5), runabout (2–4), coupe (2–4) and convertible coupe (2–4); club sedan (5), sedan (7), sedan-limousine (7), touring (7). Custom: Twenty custom bodies from previous coachbuilders plus Rollston, LeBaron and Murphy.

1929 Model 626: Sedan (5), coupe (2–4), convertible coupe (2–4).

1929 Model 633: Phaeton (5), runabout (2–4), touring (7), sedan (7), sedan-limousine (7), club sedan (5), coupe (4).

1929 Model 640: Runabout (2–4), phaeton (5), coupe (2–4), touring (7), convertible coupe (2–4), coupe (4), club sedan (5), sedan (7), sedan-limousine (7) and three Dietrich customs.

1929 Model 645: Runabout (2–4), phaeton (5), coupe (2–4), sport phaeton (5), touring (7), coupe (5), club sedan (5), sedan (7), sedan-limousine (7) and thirteen individual customs by Dietrich, LeBaron and Rollston.

1930 Model 726: Sedan (5).

1930 Model 733: Coupe (2–4 and 5), convertible coupe (2–4), phaeton (4), sport phaeton (4), roadster (2–4), touring (5–7), sedan (5–7), club sedan (5), sedan-limousine (5–7).

1930 Models 740 and 745: Coupe (2–4 and 5), convertible coupe (2–4), phaeton (4), sport phaeton (4), roadster (2–4), touring (5–7), sedan (5 and 5–7), club sedan (5), sedan-limousine (5–7).

1930 individual customs: Fifteen bodies by Brewster, LeBaron, Rollston and Dietrich offered on 733, 740 and 745.

1931 Model 833: Convertible sedan (833) added; new convertible victoria and convertible sedan by Dietrich plus cabriolet, landaulet, town car, town car-landaulet, sedan-limousine, sport cabriolet, sport landaulet "Custom Made by Packard" for 833 individual custom.

Serial Numbers
1924: 200001–208428
1925–1926: 208997–219002
1927: 220007–224511
1928: 225013–232815
1929 Models 626 and 633: 233017–276166
1929 Models 640 and 645: 167001–178879
1930 Models 726 and 733: 277013–305283
1930 Models 740 and 745: 179001–184000, 184501–187508
1931 Models 826 and 833: 320001–332111
1931 Models 840 and 845: 188001–191345

Price History

95+ point condition 1	1982	1987	1992	Return
1924 Open	$ 30,000	$ 35,000	$ 45,000	8.5%
1925–1928 Open	44,000	60,000	70,000	9.7
1924–1928 Closed	20,000	22,500	27,500	6.6
1929–1931 Non-custom Open	65,000	100,000	150,000	18.2
1929–1931 Custom Open	120,000	175,000	300,000+	20.1
1929–1931 Non-custom Closed	35,000	65,000	80,000	18.0
1929–1931 Custom Closed	60,000	110,000	200,000	27.2

Chapter 7

Speedster Eights, 1929–1930, 1934

Models 626, 734 and 1108 with Special Bodies

	Fun	Investment	Anguish
Open	10	10	8
Closed	6	7	9

Packard president Alvan Macauley and chief engineer Jesse Vincent welcomed the idea of a light, fast road car to match their company's prowess on the water and in the air. With that in mind, Vincent developed a special Speedster on a Sixth Series chassis and tested it at length on the Packard Proving Grounds in Utica, Michigan, which opened in 1927. Charles Lindbergh, who paid a visit to Packard after his epic Atlantic flight, remembered driving the fenderless Vincent Speedster at 109 mph, and in the hands of a professional it could average 128 mph. This car has recently been rediscovered and is being restored by a team of Packard enthusiasts. They discovered that this car used a Sixth Series chassis rather than a Fourth Series, which was earlier reported. (See "Vincent's Speedster—The Reawakening," by Arthur J. Balfour in *The Packard Cormorant*, number 52.)

The enthusiasm generated by Vincent's car, and some earlier and excellent custom bodies by LeBaron, caused Packard to introduce a production Speedster for the 1929 Sixth Series. Designed and built by Packard's new custom body shop, bodies were made from production roadsters and pha-

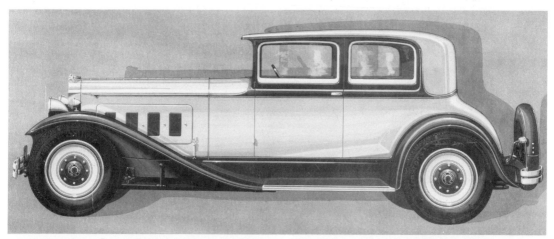

Artwork, probably by Packard body engineer Werner Gubitz, for a 1930 Speedster victoria, shows two-tone and striping patterns then in vogue—but still, blackwall tires!

etons, the roadster requiring a 14 in. cutout behind the front seat in order to fit the desired short wheelbase. It was a classic formula that would often be repeated by the industry: the shortest, lightest chassis available (the 626) combined with the largest engine (the 385 ci eight, modified with high-lift cams, high-compression heads and other details to deliver 130 bhp and a genuine 100 mph). A rear axle ratio of 3.31:1 offered high-speed acceleration; another ratio of 4:1 gave jack-rabbit starts. The 3.31:1 ratio was uncommon in those days, for it could be applied on few roads other than the Lincoln Highway. Speedsters with this axle ratio are popular for modern-day touring.

Though factory records indicate that seventy Model 626 Speedsters were built, experience suggests that the number was fewer. Only one car is known (at the Henry Ford Museum), which is a low survival rate for such a distinguished Classic.

For 1930, before the effects of the stock market crash had become apparent to Packard, a more ambitious Speedster line was planned by Ray Birge (the former general manager of LeBaron), Werner Gubitz (Packard's great body engineer and stylist) and the gifted coachbuilder Raymond H. Dietrich. It must have been like a LeBaron Old Home Week when this trio arrived at Packard, and their collaboration underlined LeBaron's strong influence on the Speedster.

Adopting a 134.5 in. wheelbase, Vincent suggested a boattail body, along with a sedan, phaeton, victoria and, a bit later, a roadster. Thus arrived the 1930 Model 734 Speedster, using Model 745 components and special bodies. Open models featured a solid brass, nonfolding windshield, without wind-wings. The body was narrower and lower than standard, and the Speedster chassis could also be purchased bare, for individual custom bodies by such builders as Kirchoff and Thompson Products (now TRW). Kirchoff built a sleek roadster with a Mercedes-like veed radiator, while Thompson produced a long, low boattail with Woodlite headlamps, a Miller-type radiator and cycle fenders. This Thompson car is rumored to exist; if found, it would be a stunning rediscovery.

The 734 engine was based on the upcoming 1932 Super Eights but was modified with a separate, finned manifold mounted at 45 degrees, a large vacuum booster and a Detroit Lubricator updraft carburetor. Two axle ratios were again offered and two

Speedster roadster, 1930, the most rakish and desirable of the early Speedster models. Chrome disc wheels were available on order.

stages of tune were now also available. Some cars were equipped with tachometers, a good idea considering their performance.

Packard reportedly built eighty-five Speedsters in 1930. The total was low, partly because of the sales downturn after the market crash, partly because such high-geared, ground-loping automobiles didn't appeal in those days. What the luxury market wanted was low-end torque and a minimum of shifting. Perhaps with other things on its corporate mind by then, Packard did not promote the Speedsters, either; Speedster catalogs are rare, though the 1930 version has been reprinted. (For details contact Robert Turnquist; see the Parts and Services section at the end of this book.) In better times, Packard undoubtedly would have

Rare photo shows a LeBaron Speedster on the street, parked in New Haven, Connecticut, shortly after it was sold. *Edward Hobart*

made a lot more of this exceptional car than it did.

Again in 1934 Packard resurrected the Speedster in a semicustom Twelve runabout

A Model 745 Speedster roadster at a Pennsylvania car show in 1978 was painted fire-engine red

with black trim and black tires: an appropriate contemporary combination. *Jim Pearsall*

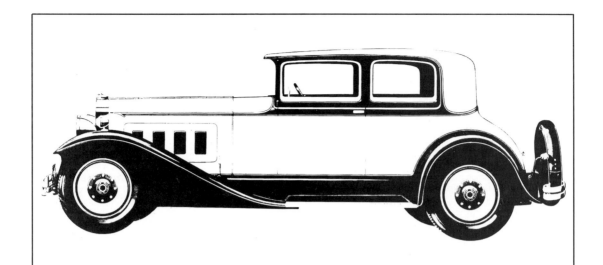

The Speedster Victoria

*M*AXIMUM *motor performance and closed body convenience are combined in the Victoria for those who prefer a fast car in a practical close-coupled enclosed design. Each of the two doors is unusually large so that the rear seat may be easily entered. Besides an adjustable driver's seat, the front passenger's seat can be quickly tilted forward. The rear seat is fitted with a folding center arm rest, and ample leg room for the occupants of the rear seat is provided by ingeniously recessing the base of the two front seats. All four windows may be lowered flush with their respective sills.*

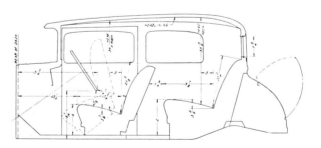

Packard artwork from its rare Speedster bro-
chure, shows the four body styles of 1929–1930.
This is the Speedster victoria. *Robert Turnquist*

by LeBaron. This was Model 1106, body style 275. Its 135 in. wheelbase complemented the swoopy, lithe boattail design. It was also expensive: at $7,796 it was the price of an upperclass three-bedroom home. Joining it was a sport phaeton, also by LeBaron, which by then was owned and run by the Briggs Body Company. Together they made a regal pair.

Alas, not many people were around with that kind of money, nor did the Eleventh Series cars mesh well with the public taste. Only three Speedsters and five sport phaetons are known to have been built. All three Speedsters have been restored, and four of the five phaetons are also known to exist. One was custom-bodied by Count Alexis de Sakhnoffsky, who sold it to radio personality Herb Shriner in 1941; after Shriner's death, the car was restored to standard sport phaeton condition, which is rather sad because it had started life as a Sakhnoffsky original.

A sixth sport phaeton with dual cowls was built in 1980 by Fran Roxas in Illinois and sold to Russell Head of San Francisco. As a *nouveau* Classic, it is superb.

Another special Speedster was fashioned by Edward Macauley, Alvan's son, after he came to head Packard Styling; he offered it as a proposed Twelfth Series continuation of the Speedster line, but this could not be justified by sales.

What To Look For

Just find one! Any one. Owning one of these elegant and beautiful Packards is more than just owning a car; it's a way of life. Even in the early 1950s, Speedster owners were writing each other lengthy letters in longhand, discussing their cars and searching for one more unknown Speedster owner. The newer owners still carry on this tradition, sharing their devotion for the model and the research.

Fortunately or unfortunately, depending on where you stand, the Speedster is so admired that more and more "brand-new" ones are infiltrating Packard ranks. It is no longer a question of right and wrong, for they are here. These newly bodied cars are beautifully built, as good as anything pro-

duced in the 1930s. In those days, profit had to be considered, but this is not a criterion today. Thus, the "new" cars are a sincere compliment to the design and construction of the originals. All good art is imitated; what concerns enthusiasts is that it not be passed off as the original art.

Problem Areas

As unique, hand-built art objects, Speedsters are not supported by vast supplies of new-old-stock parts. This is no problem, however, because virtually any body component (indeed entire bodies) are worth the trouble and expense to create from scratch. Mechanical parts are more accessible, being mainly off-the-shelf items that fit conventional models.

A major problem today is identifying an honest original from a fake; serial number plates should do this, but they too can be remanufactured.

Production

Model 626: 70 officially, probably fewer than that; only one car is known, at the Henry Ford Museum.

Model 734: 113 officially, with a known total of 85: 31 boattail runabouts, 16 sedans, 26 phaetons, 6 victorias and 6 roadsters.

Model 1108: 3 exist.

Identification

1929: Model 626 chassis with special phaeton or roadster bodywork and 130 bhp modified Model 640 engine.

1930: Modified Model 733 chassis and 640 engine with dual updraft Detroit Lubricator carburetor and five unique, low-slung body styles.

1934: Two-passenger runabout body by LeBaron on Model 1106 Twelve chassis.

Motor Numbers

1929: 166942–167012

1930: 184003–184120

1934: Numbers 902046, 902079, 902086 and 902099 known for body numbers 1108-57, 1108-62, 1108-68 and 1108-70 respectively.

Specifications

Year	Cylinder	Bore x Stroke	CI	Bhp	Wheelbase
1929	8	3.50 x 5.00 in.	384.3	130	126.5 in.
1930	8	3.50 x 5.00	384.3	125*	134.5
1934	12	3.44 x 4.00	445.5	160	135

*145 bhp with optional high-compression heads

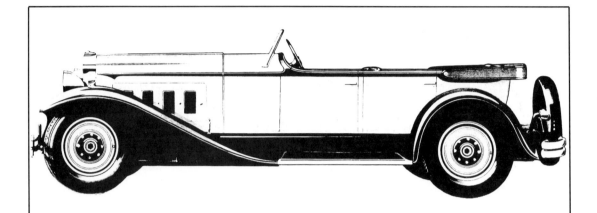

The Speedster Phaeton

*T*HE *speed of an open car, its graceful appearance and handy advantages for four passengers are provided by the Phaeton. This close-coupled design has a four-door body with the usual interior conveniences found in any standard Packard open model. Not only is the driver's seat adjustable but there is also a folding center arm rest for the greater comfort of passengers on the rear seat. As with all the Speedsters, the Phaeton is strictly custom built and may be developed in any upholstery or color harmonies that please the owner's expression of good taste.*

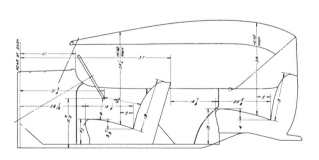

The 1929–1930 Speedster phaeton. *Robert Turnquist*

Chassis and drivetrain: 1929: As per 626 with special rear axles, ratios, differential. 1930: Modified 733 chassis with special frame sides and intermediate cross channels, front cross-tube assembly and front axle and linkage based on 633. 1934: Standard Model 1106 Twelve chassis.

The Speedster Runabout

*P*ROBABLY *the most popular body type in the Speedster line, the Runabout offers the special feature of staggered seats. Carrying capacity is two, with the driver's seat stationary and forward of the passenger to insure easy handling at high speeds. The rear deck contains a large compartment for luggage, etc., and because of its graceful streamlined torpedo design, the spare wheels are necessarily mounted forward. While a four-to-one gear ratio with low compression head is recommended, both open Speedsters may be specified with a three-and-one-third gear ratio and high compression head.*

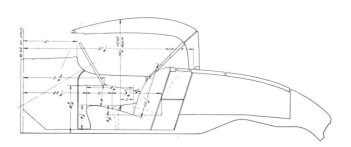

The 1929–1930 Speedster runabout. *Robert Turnquist*

The Speedster Sedan

HIGH *speeds at will plus the features of an all-around motor car, are joint attributes of the Sedan. Its low-set body bears out the appearance of swift flight, yet every detail is designed for general motoring comfort. Used as it and its sister car will be, probably more for general motoring, both the Sedan and the Victoria come equipped with a four-to-one gear ratio and a low compression cylinder head. This permits the use of regular gasoline and spark plugs, but if even increased speed is desired, a three-to-one gear ratio and high compression head may be specified at no additional cost.*

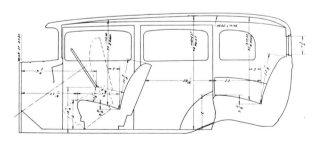

The 1929–1930 Speedster sedan. *Robert Turnquist*

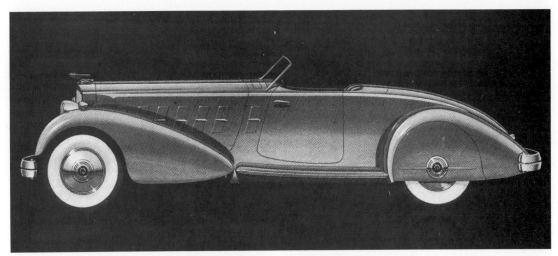

The rakish and beautiful 1934 LeBaron Speedster runabout, style 275, was one of the most desirable single models ever built by Packard. *Robert Turnquist*

Weight 4,165 lb. for 1929 runabout, 4,200–4,300 lb. for 1930 open bodies, 4,500–4,600 lb. for 1930 closed bodies, 5,415 lb. for 1934.
Bodies:
   1929: Only a runabout is known; in addition, a sedan and phaeton were alleged to have been built.
   1930: Boattail runabout, victoria, phaeton, sedan and roadster.
   1934: LeBaron runabout.

Price History

95+ point condition 1	1982	1987	1992	Return
1929	$150,000	$200,000	$275,000	12.9%
1930 Open	160,000	200,000	300,000	13.4
1930 Victoria	65,000	86,000	130,000	14.9
1930 Sedan	60,000	70,000	100,000	10.8
1934	200,000	350,000	750,000	30.3

Chapter 8

Light Eight, 1932

Model 900

	Fun	Investment	Anguish
Coupe-roadster	7	6	5
Closed models	3	3	5

Given the speed with which the Depression had arrived, we have to conclude that Packard reacted quickly. The Light Eight was purpose-designed for bad times: a significantly lower-priced Packard, the lowest since the Model C. Contrary to some observers, I believe the Light Eight succeeded in stemming the tide of economic misfortune. It sold nearly 7,000 units, about 40 percent of Packard's total sales, at a time when the Eights were doing little better and the long-wheelbase Eights and new Twin Six were selling by the hundreds. It had a base price of $1,750 for the sedan, $735 less than the standard Eight sedan, which was a huge difference in those days. And in 1933, when Packard dropped it, shifting its four bodies to the Eight line at a $400 higher price, the company hit rock bottom, selling only 4,800 cars for the model year and turning desperately and urgently to the project that would result in the One Twenty.

One could argue, as indeed many do, that the Light Eight formula would have done Packard more good in the long run than the One Twenty adopted three years later. The

A preproduction Light Eight with its simple bodywork and relatively proletarian lines that saved some important sales during the Depression.

Light Eight was every inch a Packard: its 319 ci engine came from the Sixth through Eighth Series Eights, whereas the One Twenty engine was built to a price, some say a direct crib from Pontiac. Its wheelbase was the same 127.5 in. as that of the previous Eight Model 826, versus 120 in. for the One Twenty; it was handsomely styled in the Packard vernacular; it was a lot of car for the money. Had Packard kept it in the line and expanded the body styles, the Light Eight could have been functioning as company savior years before the One Twenty arrived to do that job.

This is not to take credit from the One Twenty and its many innovations, such as independent front suspension and hydraulic brakes, but these could have evolved on the Light Eight just as easily. What could never have been the same were methods of body engineering. Building the One Twenty called for a massive reorganization and re-tooling of the East Grand Boulevard plant. And that is just the argument traditionalists use when they say the One Twenty ultimately killed Packard: it reoriented the company to a middle-priced market where, after World War II, it was overwhelmed by Big Three competition.

What To Look For

Light Eights are, like all 1925–1934 Packards, considered Classics by the Classic Car Club of America—an anomaly of sorts given

The Light Eight was handsomely furnished inside, since Packard would never compromise in that area. Factory photos like these provide important guides for restorers.

their low price, yet warranted in the opinion of many because the Light Eight remained a genuine quality car. This makes the open roadster one of the few, if not the only, open Packard from the 1925–1934 age of square-cut classic designs that can still be bought in prime condition for under $80,000. Unfortunately, roadsters are scarce; the vast bulk of production was sedans.

The handsome coupe-roadster was based closely on the same body for the concurrent Eights, except that it was shortened slightly. One-time owner Jack Triplett has pointed out that the coupe model, which had a fixed, fabric-covered top and convertible-type doors and windows, "is almost indistinguishable in external appearance from its convertible stablemate," and holds the roadster to be "the most beautiful Packard of the whole period." These two models are certainly the most desirable. (See "1932 Light Eight and Early Production Cars," by Jack Triplett, in *The Cormorant*, Winter 1971.)

Problem Areas

Light Eights are straightforward mechanically, and their problems are similar to those of the Eights. Engines are reliable and can stand abuse. Carburetor adjustments are easy although carburetors and associated parts are increasingly scarce. Body troubles, aside from parts scarcity, largely involve the wood framework, which is often dry rotted.

Production

Total production of the Light Eight was 6,750.

Identification

Light Eights are unmistakable from the front, where the bottom of the radiator is sharply pointed and slopes forward. Single bar bumpers are fitted to all models. The Light Eight sedan is lower in stance than contemporary Eight sedans.

Specifications

Type	Bore x Stroke	CI	Bhp	Wheelbase
8	3.19 x 5.00 in.	319.2	110	127.5 in.

Chassis and drivetrain: X- and K-braced channel steel frame; solid axles and semi-elliptic springs all around; wire wheels standard, disc wheels optional. Curb weight from 3,930 lb. for coupe-roadster to 4,115 lb. for sedan.

Bodies (passengers): Coupe-roadster (2–4), coupe (2–4), sedan (5), coupe-sedan (5).

Motor Numbers

360009–366794

Price History

95+ point condition 1	1982	1987	1992	Return
Coupe-roadster	$35,000	$45,000	$65,000	13.2%
Coupe	20,000	25,000	35,000	11.8
Coupe-sedan	18,000	22,500	30,000	10.8
Sedan	16,000	20,000	27,500	11.4

Chapter 9

Twelves, 1932–1939

Twin Six and Twelve

	Fun	Investment	Anguish
Open	10	10	9
Closed	8	8	9

If in 1930 you set out to design a luxury car with high performance (but one far quieter than a Duesenberg) and with the refinement of the Cadillac Sixteen (but one far simpler mechanically), you would have your work cut out for a start. But if in addition you sought to create a car that Europeans rated superior to the finest Old World contempo-

raries, you would face a monumental task. If you succeeded, you'd be able to congratulate yourself on a job uncommonly well done. Packard succeeded.

Unlike the Cadillac and Duesenberg, the Packard Twelve did not evolve from a clean slate. It began with late 1920s experiments with front-wheel-drive and a prototype

An interesting Twelve: 1933 sedan cabriolet custom-built by Packard, body 4004. This style was also available with a collapsible rear quarter or with a rear-quarter window, as a five-passenger car or seven-passenger sedan-limousine

cabriolet. Originally intended for use on the Deluxe Eight chassis in 1932, poor sales dictated its use on the Eleventh Series chassis. *C. A. Leslie, Jr.*

Tenth Series Twelve all-weather town car by LeBaron, style 759, was cataloged by Packard in 1933.

designed by Tommy Milton and Cornelius Van Ranst. Subsequent complications in the design, and Cadillac's one-two announcement of a V–12 and V–16, caused management to cancel the front-drive but retain the idea of a V–12 engine.

Most prominent among the Twelve's engineers at Packard was Clyde Paton, who followed Cadillac practice in refining the hydraulic valve silencers and a valve gear similar to those in the Oakland, Oldsmobile and Cord V–8s and the Auburn V–12. Displacing 446 ci, Packard's V–12 was a variant of the L-head, with a greatly increased angle of valve inclination to bore axis.

The 67 degree V-angle was a departure from the old 60 degree angle of the 1916–1923 Twin Six, though in line with contemporary American thinking. The quiet, rugged three-speed transmission, which was shared with the Eights, had synchromesh on second and third gears and a vacuum servo-boosted clutch.

When introduced in June 1931, the car bore the traditional Twin Six name, but this was abandoned for Twelve on the Tenth

Eleventh Series Twelve Model 1108 sport phaeton by LeBaron, body 280, appeared in New York in 1934. This car bears the traditional "ring of fire" LeBaron mascot and a diplomatic flagstaff.

Series, which arrived in January 1933. Prices began at $3,650 and ranged to $4,395 for the convertible victoria, but individual customs cost much more because the bare chassis alone sold for $3,150 or $3,450 depending on the wheelbase.

The 1933 Tenth Series had a massive new X-frame and 17 in. wheels. The 1934 Eleventh Series brought steel-backed bearings on some engines and dramatic evolutionary styling that many consider the pinnacle of Packard design in the Classic era. For the 1935 Twelfth Series the engine was stroked to provide 473 ci. Dual rows of narrow streamlined hood ventilators, a raked radiator, extended fenders forming a transverse front apron, bullet-type headlamps and more streamlining characterized the styling.

No Thirteenth Series was offered for superstitious reasons, so the 1936 series was the Fourteenth, on which changes were minimal. By contrast, the 1937 Fifteenth Series models were completely redesigned, with independent front suspension and hydraulic brakes, adapted from the smaller Packards of 1935. Also in 1937, the Bijur lubrication system was abandoned, steel disc wheels replaced wires as standard equipment and the lineup comprised three instead of two models. This provided a magnificent line of cars with a superior ride, and buyers responded by making 1937 the best Twelve sales year of all: 1,300 units.

Details of the dashboard of a 1936 Twelve sold in England by London dealer Leonard Williams. Note the dealer plate above the steering wheel. *Nicky Wright*

The 1938 Sixteenth Series had some styling changes, but basic bodies were unchanged. Alterations included a new veed windshield, an attractive new instrument panel and new body hardware; external hardware was stainless steel. Twelves now carried three adjustable louvers along each side of the engine compartment, and the radiator filler was hidden under the hood.

The final 1939 Seventeenth Series Twelve was almost identical, though it offered an

A superb Twelve Model 1108 coupe-roadster by Dietrich was built after Raymond Dietrich left Dietrich, Inc., but using his lines. The year 1934 marked the highpoint for Packards of the classic upright body style; after 1934 streamlining was more obvious.

Detail of the engine of the 1936 Twelve sold in England by London dealer Leonard Williams, including a chrome trumpet horn, which was possibly an item installed by the English shop. *Nicky Wright*

Logo of the Packard Twelve that was mounted on the front grille. *Nicky Wright*

optional column gearshift, a push-button radio and some minor design alterations. Ten different body styles were available on two wheelbases, all built to individual order only.

The last Twelve was completed on August 8, 1939, a month before the outbreak of war in Europe. It was the close of an era of American motoring grandeur, the like of which has never been known before or since. (Adapted from "The Mighty Twelve," by Maurice D. Hendry, in *The Packard Cormorant*, number 19, which was an all-Twelve issue containing eight articles on the subject.)

What To Look For

The Twelve is a nice, easy car to drive. The steering certainly isn't "power," but it is lighter than you'd expect and reasonably positive considering the long wheelbase and enormous bulk. It has a beautiful "quality feel," matched by the silken ease of the gearshift. On the road, even beam-front-axle Twelves ride well and are stable, particularly around 80 mph, which is a happy cruising speed. Despite the car's weight and bulk, 0–60 mph takes only 20 sec., which is little short of phenomenal for those times. Given reasonable care, Twelve coachwork was built to outlast at least ten owners and ought usually to be in exceptional condition on original or semi-original original cars today.

Among the greatest Twelves in the opinion of collectors are the Dietrich convertible victorias of the early 1930s and virtually all open LeBaron models. Among body styles, sport phaetons are clearly the most desirable, and priced well above even runabouts. Closed Twelves cost less and tend to be more genuine, since nobody wastes much time modifying a closed body. On the other hand, there are more open Twelves around now than Packard built in the 1930s—caveat emptor.

Problem Areas

The Twelve is not a car for the collector with few resources, either mechanical or financial. Engine work, when required, is expensive, and it is often needed because it was put off by underfinanced owners years, even decades, ago.

A fine 1937 Twelve sedan shows the changes incorporated for that model year: new one-piece bumpers, revised grille shell and rear-opening front doors. *Bud Juneau*

If the car is a 1932, a major expense is looming someday unless the engine has been fitted with a late cam, late lifters, late stroke dimensions, late bearings and an altered crankshaft. Another popular change, for late as well as early cars, was to raise the rear axle ratio to ease travel at modern speeds; this modification is invisible and does not affect authenticity. However, many such Twelves have been further modified by the

The last year for the Twelve was 1939. These models are distinguished by contrasting vertical grille bars. This Model 1707 convertible victoria, body 1227, is in perfect restored condition. *Henry Ford Museum*

addition of a radiator shroud, which is usually needed though hardly authentic; the result costs points in judging.

Among the "impossible" parts are distributor caps and spindle bearings: they neither exist nor have been replicated. Try to find a car with good ones, because the car will probably have to make do with them for life.

The Twelve's brakes will stop the car but not very well by modern standards; if they have been rebuilt by someone unfamiliar with the special shoe arrangement—two hard, one soft—the car may not stop at all.

Aftermarket, improperly designed accelerator pumps have caused many Twelves to flood on hot restart, but this problem can be easily fixed.

The Packard Twin Six Organization serves as a clearing house and medium of exchange for owners of 1932–1939 Twelves. See the Clubs section at the end of this book.

Identification
1932: Double-drop frame, two-plate clutch, manual choke.

1933: Tapered X-frame, single-plate clutch, automatic choke, redesigned instrument panel.

1934: Radio optional for first time, massive new X-frame, 17 in. wheels.

1935: Larger engine with more horsepower, dual rows of narrow streamlined hood ventilators, raked radiator, extended fenders forming transverse front apron, bullet-type headlights.

1936: Conventionally designed oil temperature regulator, chrome strip ribs added to headlights, more rakish radiator, Delco-Remy ignition with octane selector.

1937: Independent front suspension, four-wheel hydraulic brakes, elimination of Bijur lubrication system and rear-hinged doors, one-piece fluted bumpers.

1938: Veed windshield, new instrument panel, stainless steel exterior brightwork, redesigned grille and hood.

1939: Options included burled walnut instrument panel, push-button radio, column-mounted gearshift. Packard's only custom bodies this year were on Twelve chassis.

Production

Model	1932	1933	1934	1935	1936	1937	1938	1939
All	549	520	960	781+*	682+*	1,300+*	566+*	446+*

*Does not include 1206 five-passenger sedan, which was not in factory records; note large spans in engine numbers; see Specifications section below.

Specifications

Year	Bore x Stroke	CI	Bhp	Wheelbase
1932–1933	3.44 x 4.00 in.	445.5	160	142, 147 in.
1934	3.44 x 4.00	445.5	160	135, 142, 147
1935–1937	3.44 x 4.25	473.3	175*	132, 139, 144
1938–1939	3.44 x 4.25	473.3	175	127, 134, 139

*180 bhp with high-compression heads, 1936–1937

Chassis and drivetrain: Ladder type with X-brace, solid axles, semi-elliptic springs all around, vacuum-boosted mechanical four-wheel brakes (1932); tapered channel steel ladder type with X-brace (1933); Packard-built steering gear (1934); independent front suspension, four-wheel hydraulic brakes (1937).

Curb weight from 4,980 lb. on 1932 Dietrich phaeton to 5,890 lb. on 1939 convertible sedan.

Bodies (passengers):

1932 Model 905: Touring (5–7), phaeton (5), sport phaeton (5), sedan (5), convertible sedan (5), club sedan (5), coupe (2–4 and 5), convertible victoria (5), coupe-roadster (2–4).

1932 Model 906: Sedan (5–7), sedan-limousine (5–7), all-weather cabriolet, landaulet, town car and town car-landaulet (5–7). Dietrich individual customs: Coupe (2–4), sport phaeton (4), convertible sedan (5), convertible coupe (2–4), victoria (4).

1933 Model 1005: Same as 905 plus formal sedan (5).

1933 Model 1006: Same as 906 plus additional customs as follows. Dietrich: Formal sedan (5–7); LeBaron: All-weather cabriolet and town car (5–7); Packard: All-weather cabriolet, landaulet and town car (5–7), town car landaulet (5–7), limousine landaulet (5–7), sport sedan (5–7) and limousine (5–7).

1934 Model 1106: LeBaron speedster runabout (2).

1934 Model 1107: Touring (5–7), phaeton (4), formal sedan (5), sedan (5), club sedan (5), coupe (2–4 and 5), coupe roadster (2–4), sport phaeton (4), convertible sedan (5) and victoria (5).

1935 Model 1108: Sedan (7) and limousine (7). Dietrich customs: Town car (5–7), stationary coupe (2–4), sport phaeton (4), convertible sedan (5), runabout (2–4), convertible victoria (4) and sport sedan (5). LeBaron customs: All-weather cabriolet and town car (5–7), sport phaeton (4).

1935 Model 1207: Sport phaeton (5), convertible victoria (5), phaeton (5), formal sedan (5–7), sedan (5), club sedan (5), coupe (2–4 and 5), convertible coupe (2–4), all-weather cabriolet by LeBaron (5–7).

1935 Model 1208: Touring (7), sedan (7), limousine (7), convertible sedan (5) and all-weather town car by LeBaron (5–7).

1936 Model 1407: Same as Model 1207.

1936 Model 1408: Sedan (5–7), limousine (5–7), touring (7), convertible sedan (5), all-weather cabriolet by LeBaron (5–7).

1937 Model 1506: Sedan (5).

1937 Model 1507: Victoria (5), formal sedan (5), touring sedan (5), club sedan (5), coupe (2–4 and 5), convertible coupe (2–4), all-weather cabriolet by LeBaron (5–7).

1937 Model 1508: Touring sedan (5–7), limousine (5–7), convertible sedan (5), all-weather town car by LeBaron (5–7).

1938 Model 1607: Same as Model 1507.

1938 Model 1608: Touring sedan (5–7), limousine (5–7), convertible sedan (5), all-weather cabriolet and town car by Rollson (5–7), touring cabriolet and all-weather cabriolet by Brunn (5–7).

1939: All Twelves built to order; custom bodies.

Motor Numbers

1932: 900001–900584
1933: 901001–901548
1934: 901601–902587
1935: 903001–903857
1936: 904001–904719
1937: 905501–906841
1938: A–600051 to A–600620
1939: B–602001 to B–602497

Price History

95+ point condition 1	1982	1987	1992	Return
1932–1936 Sport phaeton	$150,000	$190,000	$300,000+	14.9%
1932–1936 Other open	100,000	160,000	280,000+	22.9
1932–1936 Closed production	35,000	40,000	85,000	19.4
1932–1936 Closed custom	50,000	55,000	125,000	20.1
1937–1939 Open	70,000	85,000	225,000	26.3
1937–1939 Closed production	36,000	42,000	75,000	15.8
1937–1939 Closed custom	60,000	70,000	90,000	8.4

Chapter 10

Senior Eights, 1932–1942

Eight, Deluxe Eight, Super Eight, Super Eight One Sixty and Custom Super Eight One Eighty

	Fun	Investment	Anguish
Open customs	9	9	5
Open factory bodies	9	8	5
Closed customs	4	6	5
Closed factory bodies	3	5	5

Eight-cylinder Packards except the One Twenty and Clippers are considered senior Eights; in 1942 some Clippers also qualify as senior cars, but these are discussed in a separate chapter. Senior Eights constitute the bulk of Classic Packard production and the lion's share of surviving cars. Although collectors and some speculators bid certain models way up in price during the late 1980s, the field still abounds with bargains. A Pack-

There's nothing like a Dietrich. Here is a 1932 Ninth Series Deluxe Eight Model 904 coupe, photographed at a 1970s Packard Club national meet. Only two of these are known to have been made.

Dietrich convertible victorias from 1932–1934 are considered by many to be Packard's most beautiful single model. This is a 1932 Deluxe Eight owned by R. B. Wilder of Connecticut. *Eastern Packard Club*

ard exists for almost anyone who can afford a Classic of any kind.

The 1932 Ninth Series Eight, though offering no individual custom bodies, had many improvements over its predecessor: higher compression and horsepower, standard ride control and four-speed transmission. A harmonic front bumper stabilizer was optional, and during the run Packard went back to a three-speed gearbox, which was all the cars needed given their prodigious low-end torque. A huge array of individual customs were provided on the Deluxe Eight (Models 903 and 904), which had the same engineering improvements as the standard model; both lines rode stretched

Those who hanker for Classic Packards but are floored by their price would do well to consider closed models, which are tighter, quieter and less expensive. This 1103 Super Eight Model 753 sedan was typical. *Eastern Packard Club*

wheelbases for standard and long body styles.

With the demise of the Light Eight, Packard stopped using the term standard Eight in the 1933 Tenth Series and simply called its base-line car the Eight, but it was no less a Classic than the 1932 had been. More horsepower and revised carburetion, new motor mounts, vacuum booster brakes and wire wheels became standard; pivot-pane ventilation was offered for 1933 only; and the battery and toolbox came in off the fenders as Packard moved gradually into the streamlined body. The former Deluxe Eight now became the Super Eight, with factory bodies only, having lost the longer wheelbase; custom bodies were confined to the Packard Twelve.

The 1934 Eleventh Series Packards represented the peak of foursquare Classic-era design and included, in the Super Eight convertible victoria by Dietrich, one of the most beautiful Packards of all time. Mechanical changes were in detail only: ventwings instead of pivot windows, new slotted bumpers, a hidden gas filler under the left rear taillight and a higher-capacity generator for the new optional radio. Custom bodies were again available on the Super Eight chassis,

which offered most of the same bodies as the Twelve.

Packard streamlined its bodies with a more rakish grille, pontoon rear fenders and a sloped back for the 1935 Twelfth Series, though the grille retained its trademark shape. Horsepower and compression rose again, giving the Eight a 90 mph capability. The Super Eight line underwent similar changes and comprised almost entirely Packard bodies, the only listed custom being a town car by LeBaron.

For 1936 Packard skipped the Thirteenth Series and announced the Fourteenth Series, largely a rerun of the same formula: the final appearance for Bijur lubrication, beam front axle, mechanical brakes and ride control.

Dramatic changes occurred on the 1937 Fifteenth Series. They included independent front suspension, hydraulic brakes and the elimination of the Packard Eight, leaving only the Super Eight (using the smaller 319 ci engine) and Twelve among the senior Packards. The body lineup was thinned out, fifteen styles being spread over three wheelbases.

The 1938 Sixteenth Series was similar, with evolutionary styling changes, the most

A majestic LeBaron all-weather cabriolet, style 195, on the Twelfth Series Super Eight Model 1207 chassis.

Rarely seen is a Seventeenth Series 1939 sport convertible sedan, style 710, custom designed by Darrin. Bohman and Schwartz and Rollson built similar bodies.

obvious being a divided, veed windshield. (Among junior models, the One Twenty was now known as the Packard Eight.)

By the 1939 Seventeenth Series, the smaller Six and Eight held more than 90 percent of Packard production, and the Super Eight was left with just two models in six body styles and no customs whatsoever. Though today rated as a Classic by the CCCA, these Super Eights were much closer to the junior Eight than they should have been from a marketing standpoint; the public saw this and was reluctant to pay the extra money for one.

To many observers the Eighteenth Series of 1940 was the best looking one in years, beautifully executed from the narrow, upright, raked-back grille and flanking "catwalks" to the smooth tail and tapered rear fenders. The senior line comprised the Super Eight One Sixty, with standard Goddess of Speed hood mascot and the Super Eight One Eighty, with pelican mascot. Each came on three wheelbases. This was the year that Packard began cataloging Howard A. "Dutch" Darrin's elegant semicustoms in the senior series as previously they had been built on One Twenty chassis. The Model

A perfectly restored 1940 Super Eight formal sedan displays the deft styling changes that year, notably more elaborate hood louvers and long, teardrop fender parking lamps. *Eastern Packard Club*

Darrin-bodied Packards are highly prized on both the senior and junior chassis. This is a 1940 One Eighty.

1806 Darrin convertible victoria was a truly elegant car. Another Packard first in 1940 was air conditioning, offered on all models.

The 1941 Nineteenth Series One Sixtys and One Eightys followed a lineup similar to that of 1940 but can be told at a glance by their headlamps, which now resided in the fenders, and their fendertop parking lamps. As good looking as the 1940s, they appeared

longer because Packard had not only increased overall length but relocated the radiator farther forward.

For the Twentieth Series in 1942, the model year that was abbreviated when car production ceased two months after Pearl Harbor, Clipper styling arrived on the sedans and coupes of both lines; these cars will be covered in Chapter 13. The only old-style production bodies on a standard wheelbase were the convertibles, though traditionally styled long sedans and limousines were still offered on the 138 in. and 148 in. wheelbases.

What To Look For

Senior Eights from this memorable decade exist in ample quantity. What you look for largely depends on your pocketbook, since prices of ninety-point show-quality examples range from around $20,000 for sedans to staggering highs, up to $500,000 for phaetons and roadsters, if some auction reports are to be believed. The highest prices are paid for individual customs through 1934.

In 1935, traditional Packard styling with its roots in Greek architecture began to disappear as the age of streamlining dawned. Packards inevitably became more like other

A popular professional Packard is the 1941 One Sixty limousine in funeral parlor livery. Many of these cars are available at relatively low prices.

cars, and this is reflected in collector tastes. Among custom open bodies, the highest value is attached to LeBarons and Dietrichs; among closed bodies, the 1941 LeBaron sport brougham and 1940–1941 Darrin sport sedan are much sought after.

Are any bargains to be found among custom bodies? Yes, but they're confined to the later models. The above-mentioned LeBaron and Darrin sell for a maximum of $75,000 at this writing, and a good restorable one for about $30,000. Likewise, the Darrin convertible victoria at about double those figures struck many people as an incredible bargain, soon to disappear as demand outstrips supply. Don Peterson, editor of *Car Collector*, said he thinks it's the best pre–World War II Packard buy, bar none, but expects to see auction figures at least double the 1991 level by the mid–1990s.

The Price History charted in this chapter offers few surprises. By far the greatest rise in the 1980s was among individual customs of 1932–1934; the factory bodies and post–1935 customs appreciated well but much more modestly. The lowest-priced senior Eights will almost always be the four-door touring sedans; the 1940 Model 1903, for example, was rated under $20,000 by three different price guides. So the argu-

ment that all CCCA-rated Classics have been snapped up by the wealthy does not hold water. If you can afford more than that, look especially for the neatly styled club sedans with bustle trunks, offered through 1940, and the coupes. These cost a little more, but not much.

Among those I consulted, a feeling exists that Super Eights of 1937–1942 are not the cars their predecessors were, their new independent front suspension and hydraulic brakes notwithstanding. What they lack, in the eyes of many collectors, is the magnificent 384 ci engine with nine main bearings—its smoothness and unruffled low-end torque—as well as the longer wheelbase of earlier Supers. This has also to be taken into account by Super Eight shoppers.

Problem Areas

The early 384 ci powerplant and the 1940 Super Eight—a 356 ci inline unit that topped the horsepower charts through its 1940–1950 run—were without problems. The pre–World War II Electromatic Clutch seldom operates correctly today, but most owners simply leave it switched off.

These cars exhibited few other difficulties with one exception: the 1941–1942 One Eighty's power windows, which were push-

A most collectible closed pre-World War II Packard is the Model 1907 LeBaron sport brougham, offered on the One Eighty chassis for 1941. Thin window frames were ultramodern for the time and probably inspired by Bill Mitchell's Cadillac Sixty-Specials of 1938 onward. *Eastern Packard Club*

A One Eighty Darrin victoria shows the changes for 1942, which can easily be identified by the wide horizontal flanking grille bars.

ing the state of the art, suffered from stuck windows, lazy action and leaking fluid. Trouble can be expected and if not present should be anticipated. Any car that has not had its system rebuilt with modern seals, filled with conventional or silicone special fluid (not brake fluid) and equipped with reworked cylinders is going to act up eventually.

Prewar air conditioners operated pretty much on the same principles used today and gave neither more nor less trouble than any other freon system.

For remarks on plastic trim, see Chapter 11. For remarks on pre–1940 Eights, see Chapter 6.

Gathered at a Packard Club national meet are two superb Rollsons, a sport sedan and town car owned respectively by Robert Russell and Wyatt Peterson, both of Georgia. *Bud Juneau*

Identification

1932: Standard ride control, new double-drop X-braced frame, three- and four-speed gearbox, unskirted fenders, vacuum clutch.

1933: Deluxe Eight changed to Super Eight; three-point motor mounts, automatic choke, wire wheels standard; optional automatic clutch, skirted fenders, two-bar bumpers.

1934: Single-bar bumpers, optional radio, gas tank filler in left taillamp assembly, sidemounts standard.

1935: Painted and tapered headlamp shells, elongated pontoon-style fenders, slanted radiator, new frame with extended X-member, chrome louvers on hood sides, sidemounts optional.

1936: Chrome strips added to painted headlamp shells, more sloping radiator, Delco-Remy ignition with octane selector.

1937: All seniors now Super Eights using 1936 Eight's engine and shorter wheelbases, independent front suspension, hydraulic brakes, new one-piece bumpers, more slant to radiator.

1938: Two-piece veed windshield with chrome center strip, fenders enveloping optional sidemounts, pressure radiator cap with filler under hood.

1939: Column gearshift, chromed louvers on hood sides, vertical chrome grille bars set against black background.

1940: High bumper guards holding two slim horizontal bars, optional sidemounts completely hiding wheels, teardrop parking lights on fenders complementing headlamp shape.

1941: Headlamps inset into fenders and topped by parking lights in chrome housings, horizontal speed lines on lower fenders, chrome louvers with round cloisonné medallions on hood sides, vertical "catwalk" grilles on inner front fenders.

1942: Similar to 1941 but "catwalk" grilles horizontal.

Motor Numbers

1932 Models 901 and 902: 340051–347720
1932 Models 903 and 904: 193051–194708
1933 Models 1001 and 1002: 370001–373010
1933 Models 1003 and 1004: 750000–751327
1934 Models 1100, 1101 and 1102: 374001–379149
1934 Models 1104 and 1105: 752001–753946
1935 Models 1200, 1201 and 1202: 385001–390301
1935 Models 1203 and 1205: 755001–756540
1936 Models 1400, 1401 and 1402: 390501–394505
1936 Models 1403, 1404 and 1405: 757001–758360
1937: 395501–401336
1938: A50051–A502527
1939: B500001–B506023
1940 One Sixty: C500051–C507697
1940 One Eighty: CC500000–CC503000
1941 One Sixty: D500051–D505000
1941 One Eighty: CD500000–CD502000
1942 One Sixty: E500000–E504000
1942 One Eighty: CE500000–CE502000

Production

Model	1932	1933	1934	1935	1936
Eight	7,659	2,980	5,120	4,781	3,973
Deluxe Eight	1,655	—	—	—	—
Super Eight	—	1,300	1,920	1,392	1,330

Model	1937	1938	1939	1940	1941	1942
Super Eight	5,793	2,478	3,962	—	—	—
One Sixty	—	—	—	5,662	3,525	2,580
One Eighty	—	—	—	1,900	930	672

Specifications

Year	Model	Bore x Stroke	CI	Bhp
1932	Eight	3.19 x 5.00 in.	319.2	110
1932	Deluxe Eight	3.50 x 5.00	384.8	135
1933–1934	Eight	3.19 x 5.00	319.2	120
1933–1934	Super Eight	3.50 x 5.00	384.8	145
1935–1936	Eight	3.19 x 5.00	319.2	130
1935–1936	Super Eight	3.50 x 5.00	384.8	150
1937	Super Eight	3.19 x 5.00	319.2	135
1938–1939	Super Eight	3.19 x 5.00	319.2	130
1940–1941	All models	3.50 x 4.63	356	160
1942	All models	3.50 x 4.63	356	165

Wheelbases by Model (in.)

1932	901	902	903	904
	129	136	142	147

Wheelbases by Model (in.)

1933	1001	1002	1003	1004			
	127	136	135	142			
1934	1100	1101	1102	1104	1105		
	129	136	141	142	147		
1935	1200	1201	1202	1203	1205		
	127	134	139	132	139	144	
1936	1400	1401	1402	1403	1404	1405	
	127	134	139	132	139	144	
1937	1500	1501	1502				
	127	134	139				
1938	1603	1604	1605				
	127	134	139				
1939	1703	1705					
	127	148					
1940	1803	1804	1805	1806	1807	1808	
	127	138	148	127	138	148	
1941	1903	1904	1905		1906	1907	
	127	138	127	148	138	148	
1942	2004	2005	2006	2007	2008	2023	2055
	138	148	127	138	148	127	148

Chassis and drivetrain:

1932: Double-drop X-frame, four-speed (later three-speed) gearbox, ride control.

1933–1934: New X-brace taper frame, vacuum booster brakes, three-speed gearbox.

1935–1936: Extended X-frame with tubular front cross-member deleted.

1937–1938: Independent front suspension, hydraulic brakes added and Bijur chassis lubrication deleted.

1938: Pressure gun lubrication.

1939: Steel disc wheels standard.

1940–1941: Steel spoke wheels optional.

1942: Wider frame for Model 10003.

Bodies (passengers):

1932 Models 901 and 902: Continuation of 1931 bodies (see Chapter 6) with the addition of the Model 902 convertible victoria (5). The roadster was now called the coupe-roadster.

1932 Model 903: Coupe (2–4 and 5), coupe-roadster (2–4), phaeton (2–4 and 4), sport phaeton (4), sedan (5).

1932 Model 904: Sedan (5–7), sedan-limousine (5–7). Dietrich individual customs: Stationary coupe, convertible victoria, coupe, sedan, sport phaeton. Packard customs: All-weather landaulet, cabriolet, brougham, town car, town car-landaulet, sedan-limou-sine, sport sedan, cabriolet, sport cabriolet and sport landaulet.

1933 Model 1001: Previous Light Eight bodies: coupe-roadster, coupe, sedan, coupe-sedan.

1933 Model 1002: Same as 902 plus a formal sedan (5).

1933 Model 1003: Sedan (5).

1933 Model 1004: Same as 902 plus a formal sedan.

1934 Model 1100: Sedan (5).

1934 Model 1101: Same as 902 plus a formal sedan (5).

1934 Model 1102: Sedan (5–7), and sedan-limousine (5–7).

1934 Model 1104: Touring (7), phaeton (4), formal sedan (5), club sedan (5), coupe (2–4 and 5), coupe-roadster (2–4), sport phaeton (4), convertible sedan (5), convertible victoria (5) and sedan (5).

1934 Model 1105: Sedan and sedan-limousine (5–7) now on Model 1105; custom bodies available again, same as Twelve except for LeBaron sport runabout and Packard sport coupe not available.

1935 Model 1201: Dropped convertible sedan (5) and touring (5–7), added LeBaron cabriolet.

1935 Model 1202: Added business sedan and business limousine (5–8), convertible sedan (5), touring (5–7) and LeBaron town car (5–7).

1935 Model 1203: Sedan (5).

1935 Model 1204: Added LeBaron cabriolet (5–7), dropped touring and convertible sedans.

1935 Model 1205: Added business sedan (5–8) and business limousine (5–8), convertible sedan (5), touring (5–7) and LeBaron town car (5–7); no other customs.

1936 Model 1400: Sedan (5).

1936 Model 1401: Convertible victoria (5–7), phaeton (4), formal sedan (5–7), sedan (5), club sedan (5), coupe (2–4 and 5), roadster-coupe (2–4). By LeBaron: All-weather cabriolet (5–7).

1936 Model 1402: Touring (5–7), sedan (5–7), business sedan (5–8), limousine (5–7), business limousine (5–8), convertible sedan (5). By LeBaron: All-weather town car (5–7).

1936 Model 1403: Sedan (5).

1936 Model 1404: Sport phaeton (5), convertible victoria (5), phaeton (5), formal sedan (5), club sedan (5), coupe (2–4 and 5), roadster-coupe (2–4). By LeBaron: All-weather cabriolet (5–7).

1936 Model 1405: Touring (5–7), sedan (5–7), business sedan (5–8), limousine (5–7), business limousine (5–8), convertible sedan (5). By LeBaron: All-weather town car (5–7).

1937 Model 1500: Sedan (5).

1937 Model 1501: Convertible, LeBaron cabriolet, rumble seat and five-passenger coupe, touring and formal sedans, victoria.

1937 Model 1502: Convertible sedan, business and touring sedans, touring and business limousines and LeBaron town car.

1937 Model 1506: Sedan.

1937 Model 1507: Touring, formal and club sedans, rumble seat and five-passenger

coupes, convertible coupe and victoria, LeBaron cabriolet.

1937 Model 1508: Convertible sedan, touring sedan and limousine, LeBaron town car.

1938 Model 1604: Rollston town car replaced LeBaron.

1938 Model 1605: Brunn all-weather and touring cabriolets added.

1939 Model 1703: Club coupe (2–4), convertible (2–4), touring and convertible sedans (5).

1939 Model 1705: Touring limousine and sedan (5–8). Other bodies dropped.

1940 Model 1803: Added business coupe (2) and club sedan (5).

1940 Model 1804: Sedan (5).

1940 Model 1806: Club sedan (5), Darrin convertible victoria (5).

1940 Model 1807: Touring sedan (5), formal sedan (5–6), all-weather Rollson cabriolet (5–7), Darrin convertible and sport sedans (5).

1940 Model 1808: Touring limousine and sedan (5–8) and Rollson town car (5–7).

1941 Model 1903: Deluxe convertible coupe and sedan added and touring and club sedans dropped. Running boards optional. Special airport bus Model 1903AB added.

1941 Model 1904: Running boards optional.

1941 Model 1906: Club sedan dropped.

1941 Model 1907: LeBaron sport brougham added and Darrin convertible sedan dropped.

1941 Model 1908: LeBaron touring sedan and limousine added.

1942: Only non-Clipper bodies were convertible coupes and long-wheelbase business sedan and business limousine.

Price History

95+ point condition 1	1982	1987	1992	Return
1932–1934 Open	$ 80,000	$110,000	$175,000	17.0%
1932–1934 Closed	30,000	35,000	75,000	20.1
1932–1934 Custom open	90,000	135,000	350,000+	31.2
1932–1934 Custom closed	45,000	55,000	150,000	27.2
1932–1934 Dietrich convertible victoria	110,000	175,000	400,000+	29.5
1935–1942 Open	60,000	90,000	125,000	15.8
1935–1942 Closed	32,000	65,000	80,000	20.1
1940–1942 Open Darrins	70,000	90,000	175,000	20.1

Chapter 11

Junior Eights, 1935–1942

1935–1937 and 1939–1941 One Twenty, 1938 Eight and 1942 Eight Convertible

	Fun	Investment	Anguish
Open models	10	6	2
Rollston customs	7	7	5
Closed models	5	2	2
Darrin victoria	10	10	6

Created to open a new market sector for Packard, using an embarrassing number of design and manufacturing techniques borrowed from General Motors—with the help of several key men brought into Packard from GM—the One Twenty arrived precisely on time to bolster Packard's recovery from the deprivations of the Depression.

Launched with a fanfare as part of the Twelfth Series, it accounted for 25,000 sales, more than any other single-year model except the 1929 Eight. In the annual production race, Packard rose from the "all others" category in 1933 to twelfth place in 1935 and eighth place in 1938, after the One Twenty had been joined by the Packard Six.

Most One Twentys were four-door sedans, including this fine example from 1936. *Eastern Packard Club*

This was the highest Packard would ever score, and a level it would never reach again.

These successes had less to do with the One Twenty's price—at around $1,000 it was by no means inexpensive—than with its being eminently a *good* car, offering outstanding value for money and the cachet of the Packard name, which one couldn't really put a value on but which most people thought mattered a lot. In certain engineering aspects, like its independent front suspension and hydraulic brakes, the One Twenty was actually ahead of its senior Packard counterparts, blazing the trail for them to follow.

Packard responded to a huge backlog of demand by reorganizing its plant to produce more cars than it had ever before contemplated during the 1936 Fourteenth Series. One Twenty sales better than doubled to 55,000—the best-selling eight-cylinder Packard in history. Among the important changes were an increase in horsepower to 120 (matching the wheelbase length and enhancing the meaning of the model name) and the elimination of front "suicide doors."

After the Six arrived as Packard's price leader in 1937, the Fifteenth Series One Twenty was upgraded and raised in price, and Packard opened some room above it by eliminating the standard Eight. Some of the upgrading included adjustable Marshall coil seat springs and automatic radiator shutters; a clock, sprung steering wheel, deluxe radiator and whitewalls were offered as options. This year saw the first long-wheelbase One Twentys: a touring sedan and limousine, each for seven passengers, with the highest One Twenty list prices to date, around $2,000. Another new body style was a station wagon, albeit with a proprietary body, built on a One Twenty chassis by outside manufacturers.

By the Sixteenth Series in 1938, the standard Eight was eliminated, so Packard renamed the One Twenty the Eight and extended its wheelbase. The 1938 was one of the nicest junior Packards to date. Especially attractive were a trio of Rollston customs, which were definitely not economy Packards: an all-weather cabriolet, town car and brougham, listing at $4,810, $4,885 and

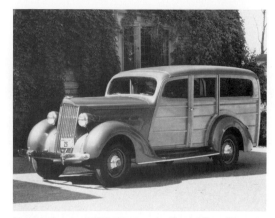

Beginning in 1937, Packard offered One Twenty station wagons, usually bought by hotels and livery services, with wooden bodies by outside suppliers like Baker Rausch and Lang. This is a 1937 factory photograph labeled as a prototype.

$5,100 respectively. But Packard kept the lid on conventional model prices, and hard bargainers could still get an Eight for under $1,200.

People kept referring to the Eight by its original name, so One Twenty was officially readopted for the 1939 Seventeenth Series. The name was used until Clipper bodies arrived for the junior Packards in 1942. The

Among closed Packards, coupes are prized by collectors for their more svelte appearance. Note detail differences for 1938 on hood louvers and the 1938's smooth bumper. *Eastern Packard Club*

This custom-bodied Model 1701A Safari Wagon from 1939 was on a Packard Eight chassis. *Eastern Packard Club*

Packard Handishift column-mounted gearchange was standard on 1939 One Twentys, with Econo-Drive overdrive and No-Rol hill holder optional. Rollston's custom bodies again disappeared.

The Eighteenth Series 1940 One Twenty shared the exquisite styling of the Super Eights, which was especially effective on Dutch Darrin's convertible victoria, a cataloged custom that was also offered on the Super Eight that year. Darrin, whose first customs had been built on 1938 chassis, told me he preferred the One Twenty's chassis to the senior's because it had the same wheelbase but weighed less.

A desirable One Twenty body style was the convertible sedan. This 1940 Model 1801 added the handsome, chiseled styling Packard acquired in that year. *Eastern Packard Club*

Body styles were pared for the Nineteenth Series in 1941. This was the One Twenty's last year, when only 17,000 were sold, the fewest in its seven-year lifespan. Styling was similar to 1940, and two-tone paint jobs were now popular on One Twenty sedans and coupes.

For the 1942 Twentieth Series, Clipper styling (see Chapter 13) took over everything but the convertibles, which were called Packard Eights to fall in with the Clipper Eight sedans. Since they retained previous One Twenty bodies, they are included here as part of the One Twenty family.

To contemplate how completely the junior Packards had come to dominate company interests in 1941, one has only to consider the proportions of the model run: 93 percent were One Tens, One Twentys or Clippers (the last only one step above the juniors). The One Twenty had now become a peripheral model, no longer the desperate attempt to garner sales that it had been in 1935–1936. But it was nevertheless a superb automobile. Mechanical changes in 1941 were few: thin-wall rod and main bearings, and rustproof austenitic steel alloy valves. Though body styles were fewer, they included more luxury or sporting types, such as the convertible coupe and sedan, the latter being the most expensive at $1,725.

Some have suggested that Packard should have named its new, middle-priced cars of 1935–1941 Macauleys, in honor of its long-time president Alvan Macauley (who rejected the very thought). Perhaps the Packard Six and One Ten should have been called something else, but the One Twenty was a Packard through and through. In the early days of the old-car avocation, when Classics cost $500, the One Twenty was derided as an affront to the marque. In the more contemplative and learned climate of the 1990s, it is recognized for what it was: one of the finest cars in its class built in America.

What To Look For

The One Twenty pecking order begins with the Darrin victoria, a cataloged custom in 1940, known also to exist on chassis between 1938 and 1942. Follow that with the Rollston customs of 1938, the outsider-built woodie wagons, and all the convertible coupes and convertible sedans built. This group of One Twentys comprises the cream of the crop.

After that, prices tail off appreciably, though the vastly upgraded, longer-wheelbase post–1937 models are more interesting to collectors than are their predecessors. The closed body styles to look for are the sportier-looking ones, like the club coupes, or the limited-production long-wheelbase models built in 1938–1939. The business coupe is as good looking as the club coupe, if more Spartan in furnishings; the prosaic four-door touring sedan is the most common and least desirable, but packs the same fine driving qualities as the others.

I have rated One Twentys high in the Fun category, because they are great fun to drive, solid, powerful and reliable. I know Packard people with Twelves and Super Eights who prefer to drive their One Twentys. As a driver's car, it is one of Packard's best.

Problem Areas

These user-friendly Packards have few mechanical problems and no parts shortages to complicate your life. Matching upholstery in custom models is difficult, as it is with most other old cars, and deluxe accessories

Packard offered air conditioning, an industry first in 1940, and continued the option through 1942. Here it appeared on a 1942 One Twenty.

Much of the trunk space was occupied by the condenser.

Two-toning was common on 1941 One Twen-tys; this car bears the correct pattern. The light color was usually on top. Among accessories were spotlights and sidemount-riding rearview mirror. *Eastern Packard Club*

has been going on, and some dashes have been repaired with filler, epoxy and paint. Inspect these areas to see if the job was done right.

The 1935–1938 models originally had aluminum heads. Any that remain may be considered trouble-in-the-waiting. If the installed head has 10 mm spark plugs, it is a replacement and should be reliable.

The 1942 models had war-related problems: cast-iron pistons replaced aluminum in some cars, and parts shortages occasionally resulted in odd combinations. For example, the 1942 line used some thirteen different sets of wheel covers. Lower grilles did not hold up well and replacements are hard to find.

like artillery wheels, fender skirts and trunk racks were seldom purchased when the cars were new, so they are rare now.

Some of the later cars were equipped with the Electromatic clutch, Packard's quick response to General Motors' Hydra-matic. Do not insist that it operate properly as a condition of buying a particular car; if it never works right, just leave it switched off.

The plastic dashboards and trim items that began appearing in 1940 did not age well. Originals were ruined by the sun many years ago. A certain amount of reproduction

Identification

1935: Characteristic Packard grille, deeply skirted fenders, one row of horizontal windstream ventilators on hood sides, front doors hinged at rear.

1936: Front doors hinged at front, double bar bumper, rear footrest part of front seatback.

1937: Four instead of five sections of hood louvers, sprung steering wheel, sponge-backed carpets, automatic radiator shutters.

Although Clipper styling was used by most 1942 Packards, One Twenty convertibles retained the older design. These are the most desirable 1942s. *Eastern Packard Club*

1938: Seven inch increase in wheelbase and long-wheelbase models in lineup, divided veed windshield, two sections of hood louvers.

1939: Column gearshift. Overdrive optional.

1940: Narrower radiator and hood, with additional chrome-plated hood louvers.

1941: Headlamps inset into fenders, "cat-walk" grilles flanking main grille. Running boards and two-tone paint optional.

1942: Flanking grilles now horizontal.

Motor Numbers
1935: X1526–X26701
1936: X27501–X82637
1937: X100001–X150267
1938: A300051–A322751
1939: B300001–B319527
1940: C300001–C328320
1941: D300001–D319000
1942: E300000–E321000

Production

1935	1936	1937	1938	1939	1940	1941
24,995	55,042	50,100	22,624	17,647	28,138	17,100

1942: Production of convertibles was a small portion, not broken out separately, of the Packard Eight total of 19,199 units.

Specifications

Year	Bore x Stroke	CI	Bhp	Wheelbase
1935	3.25 x 3.88 in.	256.6	110	120 in.
1936	3.25 x 4.50	282	120	120
1937	3.25 x 4.50	282	120	120, 138
1938–1939	3.25 x 4.50	282	120	127, 148
1940–1941	3.25 x 4.50	282	120	127
1942	3.25 x 4.50	282	125	127

Chassis and drivetrain: Double-drop X-type frame, Packard Safe-T-fleX independent front suspension, live rear axle. Multiple leaf springs through 1937; revised semi-elliptic leaf springs from 1938 on. Four-wheel hydraulic brakes. Curb weight from 3,400 lb. on 1935 business coupe to 4,245 lb. on 1938 limousine.

Bodies:

1935: Business coupe, convertible coupe, sport coupe, touring coupe, sedan, club sedan, touring sedan.

1936: Convertible sedan added.

1937: Station wagon, long-wheelbase sedan and limousine added.

1938: Club coupe, two-door sedan added, wagon dropped. Rollston-bodied all-weather cabriolet, town car and brougham added.

1939: Wagon added, Rollston bodies dropped.

1940: Club sedan added, long-wheelbase models dropped.

1941: Club sedan dropped.

1942: Convertible coupe and only model.

Price History

95+ point condition 1	1982	1987	1992	Return
1935–1937 Convertible coupe and convertible sedan	$20,000	$54,000	$ 60,000	24.6%
1935–1936 Sport and club coupe	10,000	25,000	30,000	24.6
1935–1937 Other closed	8,500	20,000	24,000	23.1
1938–1942 Convertible coupe	24,000	38,000	48,000	14.9
1938–1941 Convertible sedan	32,000	40,000	55,000	11.4
1938 Rollston custom	35,000	65,000	135,000	31.0
Station wagons	20,000	28,000	45,000	20.1
Darrin victorias	38,000	55,000	120,000	25.9

Chapter 12

Six-Cylinder Models, 1937–1942

1937–1939 Six,1940–1941 One Ten and 1942 Six

	Fun	Investment	Anguish
Open models	6	4	5
Closed models	2	1	5

In terms of individual success, the Six (sometimes known as the One Ten) was Packard's best single model. In its first year it sold over 65,000 copies, more than anything before or after and more in fact than the entire Packard line in most years of its history. In terms of image and its ultimate effect on the company, the Six was probably Packard's worst product. It took the company down the long road toward mediocrity, initially as a logical step after the One Twenty, but in the end at a severe cost.

The One Twenty could be defended: it was the right kind of car for the time, involving much less handwork than anything previous, but the only product that could save the company and still maintain what Henry Joy used to call the "Packard way of doing things." The Six was a definite step away from all that, brought on by too many managers whose experience came from General Motors, where volume was everything. Packard, ultimately, was not the kind of company to be launching a car to compete with a Dodge or Pontiac.

Dimensionally slightly downsized from the Packard Eight, the Six was Packard's lowest-priced 1937 product. This New Jersey example is a Model 115C two-door sedan. *Eastern Packard Club*

Dashboard of the 1937 Six showed replica burled woodgraining and symmetrical layout of instruments and controls. Factory photos like this can usually be relied upon for accurate depiction of production models from this period.

In the 1950s, long after the Six was born, its conceptual descendants went up against the most serious competition in automotive history—and were soundly trounced. This is an admitted hindsight judgment, but many students of the marque have argued cogently that Packard should have seen a little bit further ahead than it did. The company that had had the clairvoyance to save itself with the 1921 Single Six and the 1935 One Twenty should have also realized that the Depression wouldn't last forever. Having understood that, Packard might have also realized that it couldn't compete with the mass-volume makes when prosperity returned.

The Six was a good car. It looked like a Packard, but it had a 5 in. shorter wheelbase and commensurate shortening to the hood and fenders, along with certain cheapening devices, like two fewer cylinders, less chrome, few sporty body styles and no custom bodies. Like the One Twenty, it featured independent front suspension, hydraulic brakes, three-speed synchromesh transmission and a grille that could only have come from East Grand Boulevard.

Unlike the One Twenty, it was definitely built to a price: the bottom-rung business coupe advertised for $795, the four-door sedan, which most people bought, for $895. Sixes sold like nickel hamburgers in 1937 and, with the help of the One Twenty, gave Packard its first 100,000 unit year.

Subsequent changes paralleled those of the One Twenty. A larger-displacement engine with more torque and a claimed 78 mph top speed arrived in the 1938 Sixteenth Series, when the wheelbase was increased to 122 in. (the One Twenty's had grown commensurately to 127 in.). All-steel bodies replaced composite bodies with fabric top sections this same year.

The Seventeenth Series 1939 Six offered Handishift column gearchange and the No-Rol hill holder, and the leaf springs of 1938 had an extra leaf, like those on the One Twenty.

The evolutionary styling of the One Twenty was similarly applied to what was

An elegant 1940 One Ten convertible coupe, Model 1800, restored with one minor flaw, its whitewalls. Wider whites should be fitted: This more narrow width did not come into use until 1954. *Eastern Packard Club*

called the One Ten in 1940, including the handsome vertical side grilles, headlamps in painted shells affixed to inner front fenders and parking lights in similar small shells on the fender tops. The One Ten was a more luxurious car, with bumper guards on all models, assist cords in the sedans and robe rails in the four-door models. Warner Gear supplied the overdrive unit, when ordered.

Sales of Eighteenth Series 1940 models were almost as good as 1937, so many former One Twenty bodies were applied to the Nineteenth Series One Ten in 1941. For the first time the company offered Deluxe as well as standard models, and even an extended wheelbase for a Packard taxi. Alas, sales were only half as good, though some of the downturn was caused by people who coughed up enough extra for the One Twenty, or perhaps the new Clipper.

For the Twentieth Series in 1942 the name Packard Six was readopted, but applied mainly to Clipper models (see Chapter 13). However, the convertible coupe and station wagon, which couldn't easily be changed, retained the older styling pattern.

What To Look For

The supply of Packard Sixes is fairly good, though interest in them is relatively low. This has partly to do with a certain reputation for unreliability (see the Problem Areas section below) and also with the perception Packard people have of them as a definite step down from the luxury tradition of the company. Still, convertibles and wagons are sought after and worth considering. If you like the superlative styling of the last "traditional" Packards during the early 1940s, this is the least-expensive way to go about owning it.

Problem Areas

The late Six has few notorious problem areas, and all of the minor problems occurred early. The early versions may have overheating problems that need attention, and the Chandler-Groves carburetor used throughout the 1937 model year did not work well. The factory substituted Carter and Stromberg carburetors; present-day owners are well advised to disregard authenticity and do likewise.

Even narrower whitewalls are obviously not right on this 1941 One Ten touring sedan. Note

Special script on sides of hood. *Eastern Packard Club*

These cars, never overwhelming in power, are consequently geared fairly low and are hard put to maintain sustained freeway speeds. The advent of overdrive in 1939 was a welcome event.

Identification
1937: Similar to but shorter than the One Twenty, with louvers on hood sides stamped of sheet steel without chrome.

1938: Chrome strip running atop the hood, up the new divided windshield and onto the roof.

1939: Column gearshift. Overdrive optional.

1940: Narrower radiator and hood, with additional chrome-plated hood louvers.

1941: Headlamps inset into fenders, "cat-walk" grilles flanking main grille. Running boards and two-tone paint optional.

1942: Flanking grilles now horizontal.

Motor Numbers
1937: T1501–T67104
1938: A1501–A31660
1939: B60001–B620999
1940: C1501–C64111
1941: D1501–D38000
1942: E1501–E14000

Production

1937	1938	1939	1940	1941
65,400	30,050	24,350	62,300	34,700

1942: Wagons and convertibles were small portions, not broken out separately, of a total of 11,325 Packard Sixes, the majority of which were Clippers.

Specifications

Year	Bore x Stroke	CI	Bhp	Wheelbase
1937	3.44 x 4.25 in.	237	100	115 in.
1938	3.50 x 4.25	245	100	122
1939–1940	3.50 x 4.25	245	100	122
1941	3.50 x 4.25	245	100	122, taxicab 133
1942	3.50 x 4.25	245	105	122, taxicab 133

Chassis and drivetrain: Double-drop I-beam X-frame, independent Packard Safe-T-fleX front suspension, live rear axle with semi-elliptic leaf springs. Curb weight from 3,140 lb. on 1937 business coupe to 3,950 lb. on 1941 taxicab.

Bodies:

1937: Business coupe, sport coupe, touring coupe, five-passenger sedan, club sedan, convertible coupe, touring sedan, station wagon.

1938: Two-door sedan and club coupe added; sport coupe, touring coupe and five-passenger sedan dropped.

1939–1940: Station wagon reinstated.

1941: New Deluxe line including club coupe, convertible coupe, two-door and four-door touring sedans and wagon; taxicab added to base-line series.

1942: Bodies restricted to convertible coupe and wagon.

Price History

95+ point condition 1	1982	1987	1992	Return
Convertible coupe	$19,000	$37,500	$40,000	16.1%
Station wagon	14,000	26,000	38,000	22.1
Sport coupe	9,500	22,000	25,000	21.4
Club sedan	8,000	14,000	17,000	16.3
Other closed	7,000	8,000	10,000	7.4

Chapter 13

Junior Clippers, 1941–1947

1941 Clipper, 1942–1947 Clipper Six and Clipper Eight

	Fun	Investment	Anguish
Sedans	3	1	3
Club sedans	5	3	3

So many people have claimed credit for designing the Packard Clipper that you'd think it was an art form to rival the Dietrich convertible victoria. It wasn't, really, and except for the elegant Super Clippers (see Chapter 14), it doesn't have a lot of fans. For one thing, the Clipper existed only as a four-door sedan or two-door coupe. Packard never managed to produce more sporty body styles before World War II and didn't bother afterward. The Clipper design was finally erased by a massive facelift in 1948.

Nevertheless, the single-model four-door Clipper sedan of 1941 was a significant car in many ways. It allowed Packard to make the necessary transition from the classic body styles of the 1920s and 1930s to the envelope body of the 1940s, without losing the admirable hallmarks of Packard design: the tall, ox-yoke radiator grille, the pointed speed

This scarce 1941 Clipper owned by Gil Rebar of Warren, Michigan, had 132,000 miles on it when I road tested it for *Special-Interest Autos* in 1980. The two-tone paint job is in the correct pattern, which is not always the case. *Roy Query*

This photo shows the styling changes wrought for the 1942 Clipper, mainly the extension of lower horizontal grille bars around the front fenders.

A Clipper Deluxe Eight from 1946 or 1947, showing the wider-spaced grille bars that identify post-World War II production. Two-toning was confined to the greenhouse and deck after the war; the hood flash used in 1941–1942 was dropped.

line, the elegant curve of fender and bank-vault solidity for which the marque was known.

The Clipper was a dramatic departure, yet firmly rooted in tradition. It brilliantly bridged the gap between old and new concepts of style, avoiding blind alleys like Chrysler's Airflow. Had World War II not come along to stop it in its tracks, the Clipper would have evolved into a broad line of splendid new Packards including many open body styles. Howard Darrin proved how good a soft-top Clipper would look with a one-off convertible designed for Errol Flynn,

In contrast to the Clipper coupe, the four-door sedan's second color, when specified, ended above the deck, following the curving line of the rear roof quarter. The side window frames were not painted the second color.

and a postwar convertible sedan by Derham was magnificent.

It was Darrin, most researchers agree, who first influenced the Clipper lines, particularly the flow of the front fenders—though Darrin had wanted their line to continue straight back to the rise of the rear fenders. Packard body engineer Werner Gubitz was also involved, as was the Briggs Body Company and George Walker. But people with an eye for design, like Alex Tremulis who then worked for Briggs, insist that the concept was Darrin's.

Though the Clipper used the 282 ci L-head Eight of the One Twenty and rode the same 127 in. wheelbase, the chassis was completely redesigned. Its new, double-drop frame made the Clipper lower than any previous Packard. The rear shocks were angled, aircraft style. Clipper body construction was also different. Single pieces of steel formed the body from cowl to trunk, the hood and the combination fender-quarter panels. The floorpan had only one welded seam. The hood, hinged on each side, allowed engine access from the right or left, or could be lifted entirely free if required. Door hinges were hidden and the trunk lid was counterbalanced. The car even had a

Ventalarm to warn when the gas tank was nearly full—it whistled like a tea kettle as the fuel level reached the top.

As a solitary sedan in 1941, the Clipper accounted for 16,600 cars, which was creditable. In 1942, almost all Packard bodies used Clipper styling. This chapter is confined to the Six and Eight using Clipper bodies through 1947.

What To Look For

The 1941 Clipper, distinct from the other cars in this chapter because of its longer wheelbase, is inexpensive but scarce. So indeed are the 1942s, particularly the sleek fastback coupes, which were of much lower production than the sedans. Postwar Eights are available, but postwar Sixes are scarce; only one noncommercial example—properly finished with black tires and a conservative paint job—is known to me, and I have never seen any of the taxicabs that accounted for most six-cylinder chassis after the war.

The reason for their scarcity seems to be that these are forgotten cars. Collectors interested in the Clipper at all have gravitated toward the big, luxurious Supers. The 1941 Clipper was as large as those, but its engine was smaller and it never approached the trim level of the 1942–1947 Super Clippers.

Packard specialists are more sophisticated now than they were in the 1970s, however, so any 1941 Clipper attracts attention at

A small number of Clipper Sixes saw heavy-duty use as taxicabs, furnished with equipment by taxi suppliers.

This 1941 Clipper touring sedan with two-tone paint is photographed from an angle that missed the hood stripe.

Packard meets. A number of variations and odd two-tone paint jobs were done, and these are always of interest if they are original to the car. A taxicab, authentically restored, would be a genuine find.

Problem Areas

The 1941 Clipper is mechanically identical to the 1941 One Twenty, whereas the 1942 Clippers are mechanically identical to their counterparts with older styling, such as the Six and Eight. None of the Clippers present any special mechanical challenge. As with their postwar equivalents, the Clipper body style is most susceptible to rust along the rocker panels and below the headlights. The 1946–1947 Clippers are in most details repeats of the 1942s.

Production

Model	1941	1942	1946–1947
Clipper Eight	16,600	19,199	6,526
Clipper Six	—	11,325	30,931

Price History

95+ point condition 1	1982	1987	1992	Return
1941 Clipper	$7,200	$ 9,000	$12,000	10.8%
1942–1947 Clipper Six	6,500	9,000	11,000	11.1
1942–1947 Clipper Eight	7,500	10,000	12,000	9.9

Note: High prices for Six and Eight are based on club sedan, a more popular body style than the four-door sedan, which was the only body available on the longer 1941 Clipper.

Identification

1941: Grille composed of thin, finely spaced horizontal bars flanked by wide, larger bars extending out to under headlamps.

1942: Flanking bars wrap around front fenders to wheel arches.

1946–1947: Grille composed of thicker, more widely spaced horizontal bars that match the flanking bars, which remain in the style of 1942; ashtray suspended from lower center instrument panel instead of being recessed in the center top of the cowl. No external differences between the two model years: refer to motor numbers.

Motor Numbers

1941: D400001–D418000
1942 Eight: E300000–E321000
1942 Six: E1501–E14000
1946 Eight: F3000001–F31999
1946 Six: F1501–F14999
1947 Eight: F32001–39999
1947 Six: F15001–F50999

Specifications

Year	Cylinder	Bore x Stroke	CI	Bhp	Wheelbase
1941	8	3.25 x 4.25 in.	282	125	127 in.
1942–1947	8	3.25 x 4.25	282	125	120
1942–1947	6	3.50 x 4.25	245.3	105	120

Chassis and drivetrain: Double-drop box-section side rail taper-pressed steel frame, independent Packard Safe-T-fleX front suspension, live rear axle with multiple leaf spring. Curb weight from 3,365 lb. (1942 Clipper Six business coupe) to 3,751 lb. (1941 Clipper).

Bodies: Four-door sedan (1941–1947), two-door club sedan (1942–1947).

Eights had two levels of trim: Special and Custom in 1942, standard and Deluxe in 1946.

Chapter 14

Senior Clippers, 1942–1947

Super Clipper and Custom Super Clipper

	Fun	Investment	Anguish
1942–1947 Custom Super	6	6	2
1942–1947 Super	6	4	2
1946–1947 Long wheelbase	4	7	2

Senior Clippers are all that the name implies: huge cars on wheelbases of 127 in. or more, with all the luxury Packard could put into them. There were two lines in 1942: the Super Eight One Sixty and Custom Super Eight One Eighty. After the war these designations were shortened to Super and Custom Super. (See "The Luxury Clipper," by George Hamlin, in *The Packard Cormorant*, number 1.)

Except for cloisonné hubcap medallions on the Custom Super, the two 1942 Twentieth Series models looked identical from the outside. The difference was found indoors: whereas the Super was handsomely furnished in broadcloths, more or less like the lower-priced Clipper Eights, the Custom Super was an elaborate blend of the best Packard could offer, which was saying quite a lot. "Conceived and built for those motor-

Distinguished transportation poses at the Grosse Pointe, Michigan, Yacht Club: The 1942 One Sixty Clipper sedan, identifiable by its extended lower grille bars. Rear fender skirts, fitted to some examples, are now hard to find.

A Clipper One Eighty from 1942, with two-tone paint and skirts, welcomed passengers to its sumptuous leather and Bedford-cord interior— but how this car demands wide whitewalls! A confusion in this factory photo is the use of One Sixty hubcaps.

ists who are interested in more than mere transportation," the One Eighty was said to offer "a charm and luxury which represents the best efforts of Packard designers and stylists."

Created exclusively for the Custom Super Clipper were seat cushions and backrests on a foundation of individually wrapped "luxury type coil springs," which ensured even weight distribution and noiseless operation and were adjustable by dealers to any measure of firmness. A material similar to foam rubber was placed over these springs and into the pleats, and the seatbacks were padded with luxurious down. Where the Super employed oriental woodgraining on its garnish moldings, the Custom Super used an exclusive pattern called Amboyna burl as an applique for window molding wainscots and the central dash panel, combined with another type of grain simulating rare pearwood. Genuine leather was applied to seat and door kick panel pads. Velvety Mosstred carpeting, from New York's Shulton Looms, covered the floor and helped smother noise. Overhead Packard fitted its unique fore-to-aft headliner. The only reason given for this seemingly superfluous feature was that it afforded "an impression of greater length to the body." On Packard's top of the line, aesthetics still mattered.

There was no difference between the 1946 and 1947 models; both were designated as part of the Twenty-first Series. Though the first Twenty-first Series Packards were built on October 19, 1945, the company didn't get around to a Super Clipper until April 18, 1946. Never a high-production model, it saw fewer than 3,000 built for that model year, and the 1947 total didn't reach 7,500. No convertibles were ever built, though Derham created at least one hand-

On Dick Phillips' 1947 Custom Super Clipper club sedan from Maryland, the double-bar bumper guard trim was a dealer accessory.

A 1946 Super Clipper in side view showed how an extra 7 in. of wheelbase ahead of the cowl benefited the senior body style.

some convertible sedan that is still around. To fill this gap, Packard introduced a 1948 Super Eight convertible in early 1947.

Packard did add a dimension to the postwar line with a pair of Clippers for seven passengers: a sedan and limousine, distinguished mainly by the absence or presence of a division window. Their chassis, with a 148 in. wheelbase, was used before the war for pre-Clipper bodies (see Chapter 10). Both were offered as Custom Supers in 1946 and 1947, and were magnificently trimmed.

What To Look For

The 1942–1947 Custom Super Clipper is rated a Classic by the CCCA, and deservedly so. These are, accordingly, the most sought-after models, the long-wheelbase versions in particular, though they are more work to drive. Production of the fastback coupe was infinitesimal, but curiously, a lot more collectors seem to prefer the more common four-door model, and the value of both body styles is about equal.

Among ranks of the "sometimes available," the long-wheelbase sedans and limousines are the most desirable Clippers today, but I do not mean to discount the garden-variety sedans: these are beautiful cars, superb road machines, and many have now been brilliantly restored by Packard collectors. Yet, because they are only sedans, they are neither seriously overpriced nor commonly hyped by auctions. If you hanker to own a CCCA-certified Classic, I don't know how you could get involved for less money.

Problem Areas

Senior Clippers are well-nigh indestructible, but daily service in the Rust Belt when they were new produced some lacy spots.

Postwar Clipper dashboard was a close copy of earlier dashes, with symmetrical layout and ornate steering wheel and horn ring.

Check the area below the headlights, where there is a shelf that holds road salt and mud year-round; if that never rusted, your odds are good with the rest of the car. The rocker panels are another rust trap.

The long-stroke engine used on the Super Clippers could develop cylinder-wall taper with yesterday's oils at the 100,000 mile mark; if it has, the cylinders must be rebored.

The old fabric-and-rubber-covered wire harness is usually unsafe after so many years; if bare wire is showing, you'll want a reproduction harness.

Mechanically as strong as their conventional counterparts, the seven-passenger sedan and limousine have one major difference: their bodies were made by an outside source, Henney, and differ in several respects. Missing unique trim items, such as rocker panel moldings, are hard to find. Check any prospective purchase carefully against factory photos to be sure it has the right trim.

Packard artwork shows the underseat heater and incidentally displayed the beautiful Clipper interior and armchair seating. Amboyna burl garnish moldings were standard.

Production

Model	1942	1946–1947
Super Clipper	2,580	9,726
Custom Super Clipper	672	7,162
1946–1947 Long wheelbase	—	3,081

Identification

1942 Twentieth Series: Fine horizontal bar grille with larger bars wrapped on lower front fenders. Custom Super has cloisonné

The post-World War II Super Clipper club sedan or fastback was much lower in production and scarcer than the four-door sedan. Collector demand is about even for the two styles.

hubcap badges and more elaborate interior than Super.

1946–1947 Twenty-first Series: Wider, thicker center grille bars with flanking bars wrapping around front fenders as for 1942; no external differences between model years, refer to Motor Numbers section. Custom Super has cloisonné hubcap badges, more elaborate interior, and includes long-wheelbase models.

Specifications

Year	Bore x Stroke	CI	Bhp	Wheelbase
1942	3.50 x 4.63 in.	356	165	127 in.
1946–1947	3.50 x 4.63	356	165	127 and 148

Chassis and drivetrain: Double-drop frame, box-section side rail, independent front suspension, live rear axle with semi-elliptic multiple leaf springs, tubular shocks. Curb weight from 3,950 lb. (1946 Super Clipper club sedan) to 4,668 lb. (1947 Custom Super Clipper limousine).

Bodies: Four-door sedan, two-door club sedan in all years; seven-passenger sedan and limousine in 1946–1947. Curb weight from 3,950 lb. on Super club sedan to 4,900 lb. on Custom Super limousine.

Motor Numbers
1942 Super: F500000–F504000
1942 Custom Super: CE500001–CE503371
1946 All models: F500001–F505999
1947 All models: F506001–F521999

Price History

95+ point condition 1	1982	1987	1992	Return
1942 Four-door sedan	$10,000	$12,000	$22,000	17.1%
1942 Two-door club coupe	15,000	17,500	28,000	13.3
1946–1947 Four-door sedan	7,000	10,000	15,000	16.5
1946–1947 Two-door club coupe	10,000	13,500	22,000	17.1
1946–1947 Long wheelbase	12,000	20,000	30,000	20.1

Who says there were no Clipper convertibles? This dramatic custom-bodied convertible sedan by Derham still exists. It was built for an oil company that wanted to present it to an Arab sheik.

Chapter 15

Six and Eight, 1948–1950

Six, Eight and Deluxe Eight

	Fun	Investment	Anguish
Eight Station Sedan	6	7	9
Eight club coupe	4	3	3
Eight sedan	2	2	3
Six	2	2	5

Packard made the decision to facelift the Clipper, rather than design an entirely new body, immediately after World War II, and set to work on what latterday enthusiasts have nicknamed the Pregnant Elephants, a term of both endearment and ridicule depending on their viewpoint. It was a conventional facelift of the type that became familiar after the war. The basic body shell, which was made from the most costly dies to alter, was retained while the look was altered with new fenders, doors, hood and deck.

The vast appearance change which Packard wrought between 1947 and 1948 was accomplished entirely by these techniques. One of the stylists most responsible was John Reinhart, who told me he fought against it. "They should have stayed with the fine Clipper styling for another year or so while the strong market lasted, and planned an all-new design for 1949 or 1950."

Instead, the renovated Clipper allowed Packard to postpone an all-new postwar design until 1951, a good two years after most of the competition had restyled. This placed Packard several steps behind its arch-rivals in the middle-priced field where management had determined to fight, and put the company at a disadvantage when the real sales wars began in the early 1950s.

Meat and potatoes for Packard in those days were the Eight and Deluxe Eight, riding a short, 120 in. wheelbase inherited from the junior Clippers but powered by a new 288 ci straight eight of almost-square dimensions developing substantially more horsepower than the preceding 282. A Packard Six remained in the lineup, but only a handful got into private hands; most went to the taxi trade or the export market.

A gussied-up 1948 Packard Eight displayed accessories: bumper guards, cold-weather grille shield, foglamps, spotlight, windshield and side-window shrouds. Bumper inserts were painted, a characteristic of early production. Note that the negative for this photo was flip-flopped, making the car appear to have right-hand drive; the name on the hubcaps is reversed.

Two-tone pattern on a 1948 Eight coupe. Most Eights and Deluxe Eights, like this one, carried the stylized Goddess of Speed hood mascot, rather than the pelican, with which so many are equipped today.

Since the only Clipper shells available were the four-door sedan and two-door coupe, the two Eights (which were different in their interior trim) offered only these body styles, plus the novel Station Sedan. This semi-wood wagon had been proposed by vice president for styling Edward Macauley as a logical extension of the model package, using an entirely unique greenhouse with wood-framed windows and backlight, ash and mahogany wood panels on the steel doors, and elaborate woodwork inside.

That management chose a station wagon as Packard's first new postwar body style was indicative of how their market philosophy had changed. Meanwhile, Packard's long-time rival Cadillac was tooling up the luxurious Coupe de Ville hardtop. This was

A handsome 1948 Deluxe Eight coupe owned by Dan Petelin of California, a spotless car inside and out, was restored after long ownership by the Petelin family. *Bud Juneau*

Interiors on these Eights were stark but functional. *Bud Juneau*

the same year that Cadillac introduced its flashy new styling with the "dollar grin" grille and tailfins. In 1949, Cadillac came back with its first modern overhead-valve V-8, completing a devastating one-two punch from which Packard would never recover in the luxury market. By 1950, Cadillac was the unchallenged luxury flagship among American cars.

Despite the feverish activities of Cadillac and other rivals, Packard actually stood pat in early 1949, retaining an unchanged line of Twenty-second Series cars—the old 1948 models, altered only in serial numbers. This was caused by delays attending the development of Packard's first automatic transmission. When Ultramatic was finally ready in early 1949, Packard introduced its "Golden Anniversary" lineup and designated it the Twenty-third Series. But aside from minor trim changes and the Ultramatic option, the cars were otherwise the same.

In hindsight, and even at the time, observers could logically conclude that this was exactly the wrong game plan, what with every competitor announcing new body types and elaborate restyles while Packard hesitated. But Packard demurred for what appeared to be good reason: the postwar seller's market ran on unabated. After all, management must have concluded, we can sell everything we make. So why invest in changes?

The new design wasn't ready in time for the 1950 model year, so Packard repeated itself a second time, offering an unchanged line of Twenty-third Series cars reserialed as 1950 models. Management was finally shocked out of its inertia when a satiated market then collapsed: From an all-time model year high of 116,000 in 1949, Packard sold only 43,000 cars in 1950. Calendar-year output fell from 105,000 to 72,000.

By this time dealers were clamoring for the new car . . . but they were told they'd have to wait until the 1951 model year.

What To Look For

The Station Sedan is far and away the most sought after model in the 1948–1950 junior line. Since many of these fell victim to the elements years ago, their supply is not

An interesting junior model of 1948–1950 was the ill-starred Station Sedan, a low-selling concoction foreign to the concepts of most Packard buyers. Showstopping examples like this have been painstakingly restored; light white ash wood framing almost always needs extensive work. Hood mascot on this car was the one you received if you did not order the optional Goddess or pelican. *Eastern Packard Club*

The Station Sedan cargo area was lined with varnished plywood and metal skids; side panels were plain, but Packard applied woodgraining to window garnish moldings, as on the sedans.

large and was long ago outstripped by demand. Next to the Station Sedans, the fastback coupes are preferred among collectors, because they look fairly streamlined compared with the four-door sedans on this short wheelbase. No convertibles or hardtops were available among the Eights and Deluxe Eights. Little difference exists in demand for various model years, or for manual versus Ultramatic.

Six-cylinder models are almost non-existent, and not in demand anyway.

Problem Areas

Eights of this era are known for tanklike reliability coupled with easier replacement of small trim items than the more expensive Supers and Customs. The Station Sedan, however, offers particular problems because of its wooden body parts. Even though this was a mostly steel wagon, the side panels and tailgate are wood and therefore vulnerable. If the wood is intact, everything else can be handled. If the wood is a shambles, a first-rate woodworker will be required—you, or someone you hire. The silver lining to this is that given the talent, it is a restoration that can be done, and the raw material is readily available. Furthermore, the ultimate value of the finished car is such that the work is warranted.

Also on Station Sedans, certain unique pieces such as seat frames, tailgate hardware and license plate equipment are rare: they should be on the car you're about to buy, or the search will be long before success is achieved.

Identification

1948: Fenders and hood void of trim; front bumper forms lower section of grille;

Hillclimbing at the Packard Proving Grounds was a 1949 Deluxe Eight coupe, showing the midbody brightmetal spear and oval taillamps that identify the Twenty-third Series.

heavy chrome upper molding with Packard medallion mounted in center; rectangular taillights set flush with rear fenders.

1949 Twenty-second Series: Same as 1948 with new body numbers: 2201 Eight became 2201–9, 2211 Deluxe Eight became 2211–9.

1949 Twenty-third Series: Chrome belt molding raised above front fender openings to run length of car; Packard nameplate in block letters above front fender molding; rear windows enlarged; windshield wiper control knob on steering column shroud; oval taillights in chrome housings.

1950: Same as 1949 Twenty-third Series with new body numbers: 2301 Eight and Deluxe Eight became 2301–5.

Motor Numbers

1948–1949 Twenty-second Series Six: G–1501–G4100

1948–1949 Twenty-second Series Eight: G200001–G203000

1949–1950 Twenty-third Series Six: G1501–G1513

1949–1950 Twenty-third Series Eight: H200001–H290000

Production

Model	1948	1949	1950
Twenty-second Series Eight	12,782	13,553	
Twenty-second Series Deluxe Eight	47,807	27,422	
Twenty-third Series		53,168	36,471

Specifications

Year	Cyl	Bore x Stroke	CI	Bhp	Wheelbase
1948–1950	8	3.50 x 3.75 in.	288	135	120 in.
1948–1950	6	3.50 x 4.25	245	105	120

Chassis and drivetrain: Double-drop frame, box-section side rail, independent front suspension, live rear axle with semi-elliptic multiple leaf springs, tubular shocks. Curb weight from 3,755 lb. on Eight coupe to 4,075 lb. on Station Sedan.

Bodies: Four-door sedan, two-door club coupe on all models. Four-door station wagon (Deluxe Eight). Taxicab (Six).

Price History

95+ point condition 1	1982	1987	1992	Return
Eight sedan	$6,000	$ 7,500	$ 9,000	8.4%
Eight coupe	7,000	8,500	10,500	8.4
Station Sedan	9,000	24,000	35,000	31.2
Six	No price history available			

Chapter 16

Supers, 1948–1950

Super Eight and Super Deluxe

	Fun	Investment	Anguish
Super Deluxe convertible	8	8	5
Super Eight convertible	8	6	5
Super Eight closed	2	2	4
Super Deluxe closed	4	4	4
Long wheelbase	6	7	4

First of the restyled post-World War II Packards was the Twenty-second Series Super Eight convertible, introduced in the spring of 1947. This was a late prototype or early production car—note the license plate date—lacking a hood ornament. Backlights on production cars were slightly larger than this one.

The middle-price-range Super Eight, and its later trim variation the Super Deluxe, fell into the cracks during 1948–1950 as Packard tried to place cars in market sectors where they wouldn't compete with the low-line Eight nor the luxury Custom Eight. The Super Eight began in the 1948 and early 1949 Twenty-second Series on a 120 in. wheelbase, but this dimension made it too much like the Eight to justify the higher price Packard wanted to charge. With the advent of the Twenty-third Series in mid–1949, therefore, all Supers used a 127 in. wheelbase.

The Twenty-second Series included a Super Eight long-wheelbase chassis for seven-passenger sedans and limousines by Henney, in both standard and Deluxe states of trim. These cars sold for $800–$1,200 less than the long-wheelbase Custom Eights and outsold them handily—but apparently not in numbers sufficient to justify their continuance, and in the Twenty-third Series they were absent.

Though Packard did provide a handful of 148 in. Custom chassis for commercial bodies during the Twenty-third Series, its abandonment of the seven-passenger Supers amounted to a further downgrading of its luxury image. From 1951 until 1953, no long-wheelbase models were built at all,

A modern-day 1948 Super Eight convertible bears dealer accessories: grille screen, foglamps, bumper guards, pelican mascot, door-edge guards, gas-cap-filler guard and—in my opinion, of doubtful authenticity—chrome wire wheels. Bumper inserts have been painted body color, which judges consider permissible since this was a feature of some cars. Most bumper inserts were chrome. *Eastern Packard Club*

which sent most of Packard's commercial trade to Cadillac.

The convertible was the first Super Eight car to appear, in mid–1947, because Packard wanted to add a model with some pretense of luxury. But on the short wheelbase, it didn't look its part—especially when customers were confronted with a price tag of around $4,000, fully equipped. It sold adequately during the car-crazy late 1940s, but its mundane looks probably had much to do with Packard's decision to upgrade it.

The 127 in. wheelbase Twenty-third Series Super Eights accordingly included a more luxurious new trim variant, the Super Deluxe, distinguished from standard Super

A Twenty-third Series Super Eight sedan showed off its extra length: 7 in. more than junior cars, all added ahead of the cowl. Goddess or "donut pusher" mascot was affixed to the Super unless the buyer specified a pelican, which was confusingly but temporarily called a "cormorant" in parts references.

Eights by an egg-crate grille and a rear trim panel similar, but not identical, to that of the higher-priced Custom. Also, the convertible body style model was now a Super Deluxe rather than a Super Eight.

Super Deluxe sedans and club coupes retained the plain, woodgrained dashboard and striped broadcloth upholstery of the Super Eight, but the Super Deluxe convertible was hard to tell at a glance from the Custom Eight ragtop priced $1,000 higher. Super Deluxes outsold Customs ten to one, but we are talking about extremely small figures: Packard still hadn't done enough to retain the luxury-class buyer, who increasingly headed for the local Cadillac and Lincoln stores.

What To Look For

A Super Deluxe is more desirable than a Super Eight of the same body style. The pecking order is therefore: Super Deluxe convertible, Super Eight convertible, Super Eight long-wheelbase models, Super Deluxe closed models and Super Eight closed models. Coupes were outproduced by twenty to one by sedans, so collectors should be on the lookout for the former. There were no Super Eight or Super Deluxe Station Sedans, although at least one prototype on the Twenty-third Series chassis was built; its whereabouts today are unknown.

Problem Areas

Super Eights are reliable and trouble-free, and that includes the Ultramatic transmission, if it is properly maintained and repaired. (See "Ultramatic: The Case for the Defense," by Lloyd Storm, in *The Packard Cormorant*, number 49.)

Some special notes are warranted on the subject of convertibles. First, convertible tops are expensive to replace. Second, hydraulic systems are prone to trouble.

As in most other contemporary luxury convertibles, a central hydraulic pump oper-

Factory artwork showed the Super Deluxe convertibles for 1949–1950. Designed to look like the more expensive Custom, the Super Deluxe carried a different, lighter-gauge rear grille, and dashboard chrome did not extend across the glovebox. Super Deluxe convertibles also lacked the heavy chrome molding along the beltline that was common to Custom convertibles.

ates the top, windows and seat. If the pump works, the lines do not leak, the valves do not stick and the cylinders neither bind nor leak, then the system is in good condition and will improve with use.

But the system requires brake fluid, which is hygroscopic: it readily absorbs moisture from the atmosphere. To get rid of the accumulated water and other contaminants, you must flush the system and refill it with fresh brake fluid annually. If this task is neglected, component damage is likely.

If the system springs a leak, the brake fluid will have a devastating effect wherever it spills. It will strip paint, corrode door panels and ruin expensive upholstery. To combat this threat, some owners have been using silicone brake fluid, which is *not* suitable for this application. It lacks proper pump lubricants and causes cylinder seals to swell excessively.

If your hydraulic system does not work perfectly, extensive and expensive repair is required. And it must be done. Things will only get worse.

Identification

Series and model-year differences were the same as in Chapter 15. The Super Deluxe had an egg-crate grille and similar rear chrome trim panel; the Super Eight had a horizontal bar grille and no rear trim.

Super Deluxe convertibles, by far the most desirable postwar Supers, can be instantly distinguished from the Custom if you know what to look for. The Custom had a wide, extruded chrome beltline molding, the Super Deluxe did not. The Super Deluxe also lacked full-width chrome dashboard trim of the Customs.

Motor Numbers

1948–1949 Twenty-second Series: G400001–G430000

This is the interior of a 1949 Super Deluxe sedan owned by Ernest Benninger of Pennsylvania. Note the characteristic unchromed glovebox and plainer upholstery, which distinguished the Super Deluxe from the Custom—and an optional tissue dispenser.

1949–1950 Twenty-third Series: H400000–H416000

Specifications

Engines: L-head eight, 327 ci (3.50 x 4.25 in.), 150 bhp.

Wheelbases: 120 in. on 1948–1949 Twenty-second Series; 127 in. on 1949–1950 Twenty-third Series; 141 in. on long-wheelbase models.

Chassis and drivetrain: Double-drop frame, box-section side rails, independent front suspension, live rear axle with semi-elliptic multiple leaf springs, tubular shocks. Curb weight from 2,802 lb. on 1948 coupe to 4,100 lb. on 1948 limousine.

Bodies: Four-door sedan, two-door coupe, two-door convertible, seven-passenger sedan and limousine (1948–1949 only).

Production

Model	1948	1949	1950
Twenty-second Series			
Sedan and coupe	12,921	5,879	—
Super Eight convertible	7,763	1,237	—
Super Eight seven-passenger	1,766	867	

Production

Model	1948	1949	1950
Twenty-third Series			
Sedan and coupe*	—	8,759	4,528
Super Deluxe convertible	—	685	600
Super Eight seven-passenger	—	4	—

*Includes Super Eight and Super Deluxe models. Extrapolation from highest known body numbers of sedans and coupes suggests that only about 365 or 4 percent of the 1949s were coupes, which shows how rare the coupes are.

Price History

95+ point condition 1	1982	1987	1992	Return
1948–1949 Twenty-second Series				
Super Eight sedan and coupe	$ 6,000	$ 8,500	$12,500	15.8%
Super Eight convertible	11,000	23,500	30,000	22.2
Long wheelbase	9,000	22,000	27,500	25.0
1949–1950 Twenty-third Series				
Super Eight sedan and coupe	6,000	8,500	13,500	17.6
Super Deluxe sedan and coupe	7,000	9,500	15,500	17.2
Super Deluxe convertible	12,000	26,000	35,000	23.8

Chapter 17

Custom Eight, 1948–1950

Convertible, Coupe, Sedan and Long-Wheelbase Models

	Fun	Investment	Anguish
Convertible	8	10	6
Long wheelbase	6	8	5
Sedans and coupes	5	7	5

That Packard considered the Custom Eight to be a proud achievement was evident in advertising. Glorious brochures in full color on coated paper were created for the Custom alone. Following a Packard tradition dating back to the horseless age, no nameplate appeared anywhere on the car; the Custom was considered so evidently a Packard that no label was required. One advertisement even boasted proudly: "One Guess Which Name It Bears."

Seven inches longer in wheelbase—the difference being in the front quarter panel—the 1948 Custom bore as standard equipment a huge pelican ornament, wings upright, and a massive grille-and-bumper combination consisting of fifty-six individually assembled pieces. Cloisonné-emblazoned hubcaps and a double bar of brightmetal running along the rocker panels were further distinctions. Early models used headlight rims painted to match the body color,

Probably the "newest" Custom Eight in existence, this 1948 touring sedan owned by Don Rook had 1,800 miles on the odometer when I photographed it in 1976. This photo shows the chunky Custom's best angle.

The interior of Don Rook's low-mileage Custom shows the beautiful pleated seats, full-width chrome grillework on the dashboard and fore-to-aft headliner. Just visible at top right is a dealer accessory: a vanity mirror with frosted spots to pencil in service dates and mileage.

Custom Eight trunk compartments were lined with carpet; the "total restoration" often includes a hubcap and trim ring for the spare, as well as the other four wheels.

though stainless steel rims appeared later in production.

Inside, the Custom Eight was unique. Woodgraining was abundant; a pearwood finish panel covered a wide swathe of door area. Pleated leather bolsters and seat frames were keyed to the color of the wool broadcloth upholstery. The seats were supported by Marshall coil springs, individually wrapped in fiber and topped with foam rubber on the seat cushion. Seatbacks were stuffed with soft down. The foam-backed cut-pile Mosstred carpet was the best money could buy.

The Custom Eight convertible victoria was upholstered in top-grain leather or combinations of leather and Bedford cloth. Unique to the closed cars were window regulator handles consisting of ten individual pieces, and four inside courtesy lights plus two individual reading lamps were installed.

Attention to detail didn't stop with styling. The Custom Eight had the lowest spring rates of any car in its class, ensuring a wonderfully smooth ride; yet handling was good, assisted by a fifth shock absorber in the rear stabilizer bar to eliminate side tremor. The transmission had nine roller bearings; Cadillac used only six. Brake hubs were steel with lifetime cast-iron linings, and the chassis alone cost $3 million in development. So strong was the frame that a Custom Eight convertible could be driven quite casually on three wheels. It was the most solidly constructed convertible in the industry, the car other makers tore apart when they wanted to know "how it was done."

The 160 bhp, 356 ci eight with nine main bearings now featured only in the Custom was worthy of its role. The crankshaft alone weighed 105 lb., the complete engine nearly 1,000 lb., 150 lb. more than the Super Eight's 327 ci engine. Hydraulic valve lifters and bolted instead of forged crankshaft counterweights were *de rigueur*. The engine used only 2488 rpm per mile, idled at a whisper, cruised effortlessly at 90 mph. One couldn't ask more of a grand luxe carriage in 1948, and it would be hard to match the Custom's smooth silence today. More than any other postwar Packard it lived up to the old slogan dating back to the 1912 Six: "Soft-Spoken

Boss of the Road." (See "The Postwar Customs," by Richard M. Langworth, in *The Cormorant*, Fall 1971.)

Aside from acquiring standard Ultramatic transmission, the late 1949 and 1950 Twenty-third Series Custom Eights were little changed from the Twenty-second Series versions. Trim variations are discussed in the Identification section following.

What To Look For

Custom Eight coupes were built in infinitesimal quantities and are worth considerably more, in comparable condition, than the sedans. Convertible victorias are by far the most desirable, but plenty of people are also shopping for long-wheelbase models, though they are scarce. The most impressive interiors are red, though blues, greens and browns were also available. Because some Customs received limited use when new, a larger percentage of original, low-mileage examples exist, and these naturally command a premium price.

The restoration of a badly deteriorated Custom Eight is a formidable undertaking. Duplicating all those square yards of fine leather and broadcloth will tie up a lot of money, and an expert will be needed to construct and fit the fore-to-aft headliner, which Twenty-second Series Customs inherited from the 1946–1947 Custom Super Clippers. So many restored or original cars are around that there is usually a wide choice, at least among four-door sedans. My advice on this model is to buy the best exam-

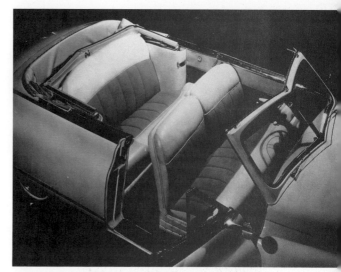

The Custom Eight convertible featured leather-and-Bedford-cord or all-leather upholstery, heavy chrome sill moldings and hydraulic window lifts, all standard.

ple you can afford and avoid drastic restoration.

The production figures include some bare chassis. These were provided to outside builders, mainly Henney, for construction of professional bodies. (See Chapter 28.)

Problem Areas

Mechanically, Custom Eights with the three-speed transmission are the functional equivalents of their Custom Super Clipper predecessors from 1946–1947. The major

Seen from behind is the elaborate Custom Eight grille, composed of numerous stainless-steel and pot-metal sections. All have to be individu-ally restored after disassembly. Grille shells, all pot metal, are now difficult to find in perfect condition.

Whereabouts unknown: a special Custom Eight convertible sedan, custom-bodied by Worblaufen of Germany, with a heavy Teutonic top characteristic of open Mercedes.

difference lies in Ultramatic Drive automatic transmission of 1949–1950. If the transmission still has the outmoded Type A fluid from the early 1950s, it will surely need changing, yet new fluid may cause leaks and lead to a teardown.

Parts for this Ultramatic are easy to obtain, particularly compared to parts for contemporary competitors, but knowledgeable service is harder to come by. Overhaul techniques that get by on other makes will not suffice for the Ultramatic. For example, the transmission is dependent on pressures, governed among other things by internal bushings. Check for burned fluid, a slipping or nonengaging direct-drive clutch or even the presence of another make of transmission! Don't laugh; switches have been made, and are being made; unless another trans-

mission is what you want, the cost of restoring the proper unit will be high.

For cars equipped with hydraulic windows, see comments on this subject in Chapter 16.

On closed Customs long in storage, you may encounter moth damage, since the material used inside was 100 percent wool. Look for it, and if you do not find it, guard against it with mothballs or more modern and less smelly moth repellants.

The pearwood door panel appliques were lacquered when new, and this coating is liable to become clouded with age. If it is, the only answer is to remove the coating with an appropriate chemical solvent. Experiment with solvents on an obscure corner of a panel before going to work wholesale.

Production

Model	1948	1949	1950
Twenty-second Series			
Sedan and coupe	5,936	2,990	—
Convertible	1,105	213	—
Long wheelbase	230	50	—
Bare chassis	1,941	220	—
Twenty-third Series			
Sedan and coupe	—	973	707
Convertible	—	160	244

Identification

Cloisonné hubcap badges; unique foambacked cut-pile Mosstred carpet, fore-to-aft

Packard returned to the limousine business with the 1948s. Bodies for these stretched-wheelbase cars were constructed by Henney.

The seven-passenger sedan was identical, except for the absence of an interior division window.

The Custom Eight as revised for the 1949–1950 Twenty-third Series featured a single body molding and oval taillamps. These Customs are much scarcer than the Twenty-second Series cars. Ultramatic was listed as an option but usually fitted.

headliner (Twenty-second Series only), color-keyed broadcloth upholstery with tan piping and leather bolsters on closed models; chrome ribbing over glovebox door; wide chrome-plated beltline molding on convertibles; egg-crate grille motif front and rear.

Twenty-second Series: Double bands of brightmetal low on body sides and oblong taillights flush with fenders.

Twenty-third Series: Single brightmetal strip mid-height on body sides, oval taillights in chrome housings, Ultramatic standard.

Note: Model year is determined by body number prefixes: 1949 Twenty-second Series uses 1948 number with the addition of –9; 1950 Twenty-third Series uses 1949 number with the addition of –5.

Specifications

Engines: L-head Eight, 356 ci (3.50 x 4.63 in.), 160 bhp at 3600 rpm.

Wheelbase: 127 in.; 148 in. on seven-passenger models.

Chassis and drivetrain: Double-drop frame, box-section side rails, independent front suspension, live rear axle with semi-elliptic multiple leaf springs, tubular shocks. Curb weight 4,000 to 5,000 lb.

Bodies:

Twenty-Second Series: Two-door club coupe, four-door sedan, long-wheelbase sedan and limousine, two-door convertible.

Twenty-Third Series: Two-door club coupe, four-door sedan, two-door convertible.

Motor Numbers

1948–1949 Twenty-second Series: G600001–G612000

1949–1950 Twenty-third Series: H600001–H603000

Price History

95+ point condition 1	1982	1987	1992	Return
1948–1949 club sedan	$ 8,000	$12,000	$17,500	16.9%
1948–1949 long wheelbase	9,500	25,000	30,000	25.9
1948–1950 touring sedan	7,000	10,000	14,000	14.9
1948–1950 convertible	14,000	28,000	45,000	26.3

Chapter 18

Junior Models, 1951–1954

200, 200 Deluxe, Clipper, Clipper Deluxe, Clipper Deluxe Sportster, Clipper Super and Clipper Super Panama

	Fun	Investment	Anguish
Standard and Deluxe closed	2	1	3
1954 Super closed	2	2	3
1953–1954 Sportster	4	7	3
1954 Super Panama	6	7	3

Packard continued to use series nomenclature until the very end in 1958, but after 1950, series were exactly in line with model years, so they are omitted from mention henceforth.

As determined as ever since 1935 to score in the medium-priced field, Packard offered a five-car lineup of downmarket 200s to replace the old Eight on its completely restyled 1951 range. Like the Eight, the 200 offered a sedan and club sedan, each in standard or Deluxe trim; the fifth model was a business coupe rather than a Station Sedan. Packard was now without a station wagon, a critical problem if it meant to compete in the mid-priced sector during the 1950s.

Basic Packard transportation for 1951 was this 200 four-door sedan, owned by a New England collector. Whitewalls are a shade too narrow for 1951; spearlike mascot was standard on the 200. When fitted, Ultramatic was so noted in rear fender script. *Eastern Packard Club*

By 1953, the low-priced 200 had become the Clipper. Tall, narrow taillights, fully wrapped backlight and heavy chrome headlamp rims were standard; pelican mascot and door-edge guards were optional. Narrow-band whitewalls are inappropriate on all Packards, since they did not come into general use until 1962. *Eastern Packard Club*

The detrimmed business coupe didn't appeal to many, and it was summarily axed in 1952, a year of shortages and production quotas caused by the Korean War. Against a good run of about 70,000 Model 200s in 1951, Packard was able to produce only about 47,000 in 1952.

New company president James J. Nance arrived in 1952 to take over from the Hugh Ferry, the former treasurer who had filled in 1949 when George Christopher, founder of the One Twenty, was dismissed and Alvan Macauley, the president-become-chairman, retired. Ferry was an upstanding,

A 1954 Clipper sedan showed the most obvious styling difference for that year: Dick Teague's "thumb" taillights, which were visible from virtually every angle. Note also the revised hubcaps and Clipper door script.

forthright executive but admitted he was not cut out for the presidency, and helped recruit Nance, who had many bold ideas. Nance, who had made a reputation as a sales expert with the Hotpoint appliance firm, brought in a new management team and moved fast to sack or retire anyone whose thinking didn't match his.

A marketing man above all else, Nance immediately saw the impact of Packard's continuing emphasis on medium-priced cars, but he didn't want to opt out of the market either. He resurrected the name Clipper to replace 200 on the 1953 line, and planned ultimately to evolve Clipper as a separate make, divorcing the cut-rate business from the revered name of Packard.

The 1953 Clipper used a larger engine than the 200. Bodies were confined to two- and four-door sedans. A trim variation on the two-door body was the Sportster, a Clipper Deluxe with special trim and two-tone paint. The Sportster was a kind of ersatz hardtop, but Packard had had a genuine hardtop available on the 122 in. wheelbase since 1951—it is a mystery why it didn't tool a 200 or Clipper hardtop earlier.

A major restyle and a new overhead-valve V-8 engine were planned for 1954, but numerous problems put these off: Packard lost its body supplier when the Briggs Company, which had built its bodies since 1940, sold out to Chrysler; a complicated purchase of Studebaker was also in the cards. Hastily, a slightly facelifted line of Clippers was fielded with few changes other than stylist Dick Teague's unique "sore thumb" taillights, which were visible from the rear, sides, even overhead.

The bottom line was now called the Clipper Special. The Clipper Deluxe was retained and a more luxurious series of Clipper Supers was added. Within the Super line was the long-awaited hardtop, christened Panama. It was a handsome car with pretty, leather and vinyl interiors color keyed to the paint job, which was usually a two-tone. A small number of Clipper chassis were furnished builders like Henney for the commercial body business. (See Chapter 28.)

The effect of Nance's management was readily apparent in the way the statistics turned around during 1953. Net profit in the first quarter was $3.5 million against $1.2 million in the same period of 1952; sales were up 182% and $10 million in pre-tax earnings was the best in Packard history. But the market slumped in mid–1953, and worsened for independents when GM and Ford declared a sales war, shipping huge quantities of unordered cars to dealers and forcing them to discount madly to keep ahead of inventories. This the independents and Chrysler couldn't match. Sales were dreadful in 1954, and Packard began to slide downhill for the last time.

The Super Panama was the Clipper's first hardtop, in 1954. Two-tone paint jobs were typical.
Richard Quinn

What To Look For

Collectors always prefer the sporty models, but these usually had the lowest production. Sportsters are hotly sought after, but only a handful are known to exist. The Super Panama hardtop is more common, and commands the highest prices among cars in this chapter. There is little to choose from among workaday sedans and club coupes, and virtually no interest in the oddball 1951 business coupe despite its rarity.

Problem Areas

The 200s and Clippers are mechanically strong but subject to rust: check the rear wheel openings, rocker panels, areas above the wheels, and the trailing lower edges of the front fenders. These Briggs bodies were built with multiple layers of steel for strength, but this construction method also created salt pockets.

Chrome on 1952 and 1953 models lacked nickel content because of Korean War shortages, thus pot-metal parts pitted early. New-old-stock replacements are scarce, and re-plating a complete grille could consume the best part of $1,000. Upholstery is impossible to replace with authentic materials, unless it is leather or vinyl; if it's cloth, just come as close as you can.

The late 1954 models have an interim-version Ultramatic transmission called Gear-Start Ultramatic, which is trouble-prone and should be overhauled to 1956 standards.

Production

1951 Model 200: 24,310; Model 200 Deluxe: 47,052.

1952: Total production: 46,720.

Packard records list only these figures for 1951–1952.

	1953	1954
Four-door sedan	23,126	—
Special four-door sedan	—	970
Club sedan	6,370	—
Special club sedan	—	912
Deluxe Sportster	3,672	1,336
Deluxe four-door sedan	26,027	7,610
Deluxe club sedan	4,678	1,470
Super four-door sedan	—	6,270
Super club sedan	—	887
Super Panama hardtop	—	3,618
Bare chassis	301	120

Identification

1951 Model 200: One-piece curved windshield, Packard name in block letters across hood front, oval grille center formed by two chrome curving horizontal bars.

Top of the Clipper line in 1954 was the Super Panama hardtop, virtually always finished in two-tone paint combinations. A handsome, clean-lined, sporty Clipper, the 1954 Panama is sought after, but scarce.

1951 Model 200 Deluxe: Chrome wheel rings and directional signals.

1952 Model 200: Name removed from hood, chrome molding across front fenders and front doors.

1952 Model 200 Deluxe: Chrome wheel rings.

1953 Clipper: Enlarged backlight, rear speed line deleted, new grille with single bar running to two large parking lights, new impact bar bumpers, deep headlamp rims.

1953 Clipper Deluxe: Full-length stainless steel strip incorporating Packard crest and chrome taillight extension.

1954 Clipper: Bottom-line model named Special. New top-line Super models including Panama hardtop. Distinctive thumb-shaped taillights at tops of rear fenders visible from three sides and above, black instead of red hexagon emblems.

1954 Clipper Special: Chrome trim does not extend through door panel, Clipper script below trim on rear fenders.

1954 Clipper Deluxe: Chrome trim runs the length of the body, Clipper block letters above body trim, identification on deck lid.

1954 Clipper Super: Chrome fender trim length of body, model identification on deck lid.

Motor Numbers
1951 Model 200: J200001–J280000
1952 Model 200: K200001–K250000
1953 Clipper: L200001–L250000
1953 Clipper Deluxe: L300001–L330920
1954 Clipper Special: M200001–M202000
1954 Clipper Deluxe and Super: M300001–up

Specifications

Year	Model	Bore x Stroke	CI	Bhp	Wheelbase
1951–1952	All	3.50 x 3.75 in.	288	135	122 in.
1953	Standard	3.50 x 4.25	327	150	122
1953	Deluxe	3.50 x 4.25	327	160	122
1954	Special	3.50 x 4.25	327	150	122
1954	Deluxe and Super	3.50 x 4.25	327	165	122

Chassis and drivetrain: Pressed steel I-beam with X-member, independent front suspension, live rear axle with semi-elliptic multiple leaf springs, tubular shocks. Curb weight from 3,550 lb. on 1951 business coupe to 3,950 lb. on 1954 Deluxe club sedan.

Bodies:

1951: Four-door sedan, club sedan and business coupe.

1952–1953: Four-door sedan and club sedan.

1954: Four-door sedan, club sedan and two-door hardtop.

Price History

95+ point condition 1	1982	1987	1992	Return
1951–1952 200	$4,000	$6,500	$ 7,500	13.4%
1953–1954 sedans	4,000	7,000	9,000	17.6
1953–1954 Deluxe Sportster	5,000	8,000	10,000	14.9
1954 Super Panama	5,350	8,500	12,000	17.5

Chapter 19

Packard Hardtops and Convertibles, 1951–1954

1951–1953 Mayfair, 1954 Pacific and 1951–1954 Convertible

	Fun	Investment	Anguish
Convertible	7	6	3
Pacific	5	5	3
Mayfair	5	4	3

Among the various rationales that governed the all-new Twenty-fourth Series of 1951 was former president George Christopher's concept of model hierarchy: one engine block in three displacements with hydraulic lifters. This was a dramatic change from pre-World War II practice when the models were based on engines (Six, Eight, Super Eight, Twelve). Christopher had reduced Packard to only three bodies: a two-door and a pair of four-door sedans. But competitive pressures forced Packard to build a hardtop, and the

Was a 200 convertible ever made? Packard experts are divided, but it seems likely that a handful were produced. Lack of grille teeth would immediately identify one. From this shot we might conclude that at least one was produced—but the photo shows signs of airbrushing, and a doodler may have been playing with the toothless look on a photo of a standard 250.

A 1952 Mayfair hardtop was typically two-toned, with triple "bottle openers" on the rear fenders and Clipper-style vertical taillamps. Pel-ican mascot with semi-erect wings was peculiar to the 1952 models.

company also wanted to restore a convertible to the line as soon as possible. Packard did both with the Model 250 in 1951.

The new body styles made their debut on March 16, 1951, the hardtop named Mayfair after the fashionable London district. They were curious amalgams of junior and senior components: although they used the senior 327 straight eight, they were mounted on the junior 122 in. wheelbase. The short wheelbase was probably a mistake, because the most competitive convertible—Buick's

California distributor Earle C. Anthony promoted 1954 Packard Pacific hardtops in special Carnation and Amethyst (white and light purple) color schemes; custom Amethyst badges were fitted, and even wheelwells were so painted. *Bud Juneau*

Roadmaster, priced almost the same as the 250—had a 126 in. wheelbase and was 300 lb. heavier—weight was no enemy in those days. The 250 had a visual as well as dimensional disadvantage, in that it carried the taillights and trim from the lowest-priced 200 series. (Refer to "The Schizophrenic 250," by George Hamlin, in *The Packard Cormorant*, number 42.)

On the positive side, the lighter body combined with the 327 in. engine gave the Mayfair, especially, excellent performance and roadability, in which respects the 250s were probably the best cars Packard had. They were beautifully furnished on the inside using lots of leather, and the Mayfair's headliner carried the fashionable brightmetal bows that were meant to suggest a convertible top. Bright colors were the rule and most Mayfairs were two-toned.

In subsequent years, Packard tried to disguise the plebian body with longer side strips and pods housing senior-style taillights. Dealers were encouraged to install the optional continental spare tire, which added length. The 250 designation was dropped after 1952, when the two cars were given a special chassis designation 2531, instead of the 2501 of the 200 series.

By 1954, the convertible and hardtop, now renamed Pacific, had received the top-of-the-line 359 ci engine, and achieved the image they should have had from the beginning. Packard was thus able to raise their prices considerably. Base prices had been about $3,300 and $3,500 for the hardtop and convertible, respectively, in 1953; in 1954 they were, respectively, $3,827 and $3,935. Unfortunately, 1954 was one of the worst years in company history, and sales of both models barely surpassed 2,000.

The fastidious should note that Convertible was spelled with a capital C by Packard when referring to the 1951–1954 models.

What To Look For

A distinct difference in value used to exist between early and late models, but this has mainly disappeared; in 1991, the buyer of a prime, ninety-point car could expect to pay around $14,000 for a hardtop and as much as $24,000 for a convertible, regardless of year. Because the cars are scarce to begin with, what you get is liable to depend on what's around.

In early 1951, Packard toyed with the idea of introducing both cars in the 200 series, and a handful appear to have actually been built. They are distinguished by the lack of side chrome and absence of grille teeth. Finding one would be a coup.

The most interesting production variation is the 1954 Pacific finished in Carnation and

Peaked headlamp rims were present on all 1954 senior Packards. *Bud Juneau*

Interior of the 1954 Packard Pacific hardtop in the special Carnation and Amethyst color scheme. *Bud Juneau*

Back-up lamps were built into the taillights on the 1954 senior Packards. *Bud Juneau*

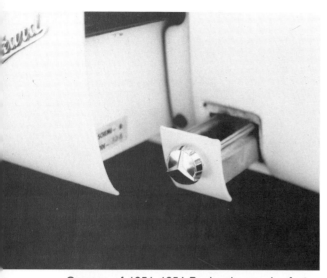

Owners of 1951–1954 Packards may be fortunate enough to discover the paint and trim codes pasted to the side of the drawer-style glovebox. These codes can be interpreted to give you the correct color and trim schemes. Slide-out ashtrays were on both sides of the 1954 dash. *Bud Juneau*

Amethyst (white and purple). The Amethyst color was repeated in the horn-button medallion and the emblems on hood, deck and rear roof pillars, and the same color paint was used on the wheels and under the fenders. When such a car was displayed at the famous Earle C. Anthony showrooms in California, mirrors were placed underneath to show off the undercarriage. Carnation and Amethyst factory originals must carry paint scheme R and trim code 324; if not, they were originally painted in different colors.

Problem Areas

The 1951–1953 Mayfairs and Convertibles are the functional equivalent of the Patricians of the same era, though they have engines with fewer main bearings; all comments about Patricians apply, as they do to 1954s, which shared the Patrician engine. Equally applicable are the special notes on convertibles found in the Problem Areas section of Chapter 16.

The 1954 Packard Convertible was the most elaborate version of the 1951–1954 ragtops other than the Caribbean, but these cars are scarce.

Identification

1951: Chrome strip across front fenders and doors, three chrome "bottle opener" ornaments on rear fenders with Ultramatic script under third one on automatic models. Packard name in block letters on hood, hood mascot with upswept wings.

1952: Same side molding as in 1951, "bottle openers" now elongated, name deleted from hood, hood mascot wings swept straight back.

1953: Full-length bodyside molding, small chrome fins over taillights, grille lacking "teeth" and having single center bar with dual fluted sections, wings folded on mascot.

1954: Side molding from front fender to behind door; three small chrome flashes on leading edge and low chrome molding on rear fender; peaked headlamp rims; chrome pods housing senior taillights.

Motor Numbers

1951: J400001–J425000
1952: K400001–K424420
1953: L400001–L418552
1954: M600001–M605618

Production

Model	1951*	1952*	1953	1954
Mayfair	1,251	3,959	5,150	—
Pacific	—	—	—	1,189
Convertible	2,001	963	1,518	750

*As roster-keeper for the 250 series, Edward J. Ostrowski has examined serial numbers of 1951–1952 models in an attempt to break down hardtop versus convertible production, which was not stated individually by Packard. The figures shown are estimates based on the highest known serial numbers for the two body styles, which account for 70 percent of 1951 models and 95 percent of 1952 models. The official Packard totals were 4,640 for 1951 and 5,201 for 1952. Ostrowski welcomes additions to his roster (see Parts and Services section at the end of this book).

Specifications

Year	Model	Bore x Stroke	CI	Bhp	Wheelbase
1951–1952	Manual shift	3.50 x 4.25 in.	327	150	122 in.
1951–1952	Ultramatic	3.50 x 4.25	327	155	122
1953	All models	3.50 x 4.25	327	180	122
1954	All models	3.56 x 4.25	359	212	122

Chassis and drivetrain: Pressed steel I-beam with X-member, independent front suspension, live rear axle with semi-elliptic multiple leaf springs, tubular shocks. Curb weight: 3,800 lb. on 1951–1953 Mayfair, 4,000 lb. on 1951–1953 Convertible, 4,100 lb. on 1954 Pacific, 4,300 lb. on 1954 Convertible.

Bodies: Two-door hardtop and two-door convertible.

Price History

95+ point condition 1	1982	1987	1992	Return
1951–1952 Mayfair hardtop	$ 5,500	$ 9,000	$12,000	16.9%
1951–1952 Convertible	7,800	13,000	20,000	20.7
1953 Mayfair hardtop	6,200	9,000	13,000	16.0
1954 Pacific hardtop	7,500	9,500	14,000	13.3
1953–1954 Convertible	10,000	17,000	24,000	19.1

Chapter 20

Medium-Priced Sedans, 1951–1954

300 and Cavalier

	Fun	Investment	Anguish
All	2	3	3

These four-door sedans occupied the market sector formerly held by the old Super Eight, above the 200 or Clipper and below the Patrician. In 1951 and 1952, they were known as the 300; in 1953 and 1954, they were referred to as the 300 or Cavalier, or both.

For about $600 less than the cost of a Patrician, the 300 and Cavalier offered the Patrician's commodious interior and long wheelbase with about the same performance; the traditional-minded could even order a 300 or Cavalier with manual transmission, with or without overdrive. A number of bare chassis were furnished commercial builders (see Chapter 28).

These cars lacked the magnificent luxury interiors of the Patricians, being done up in conventional striped broadcloths, but nothing was cheap about the way they were built. In 1953–1954, they were grouped by Packard with the Mayfair, Pacific and Convertible, which were said to be "sporty models of the Cavalier."

What To Look For

The 300 and Cavalier are big, comfortable, road-gobbling six-passenger cars, which competed in their day with the Buick Roadmaster, DeSoto, Oldsmobile 98 and Lincoln Cosmopolitan. They have fallen through the cracks among collectors because they lack

A toothy grille and long wheelbase marked the 1951 Model 300, a detrimmed Patrician that sold at a much lower price. Rear fenders bear Ultra-matic script on this model; Packard's automatic was standard only on the Patrician that year.

For 1952, the 300 was carried over with few changes except for the distinctive pelican mascot. The 300 script on the rear roof quarters is usually found on all 1951 and some 1952 cars, but appears to have disappeared early in the 1952 model year.

the gilt-edged panache of the Patrician and the sporty body styles of the Mayfair, Pacific and Convertible. As a result, you can pick one up for a small price, though survival rates are low. Production in 1954 was way down and the 300 or Cavalier was outproduced by the Patrician, so if you have a choice, this is the model year to look for. The 1953 and 1954 models have somewhat more power than the earlier versions.

Problem Areas

The 300 and Cavalier are sound cars but susceptible to rust. Check especially rear

The 300 interiors were stark by comparison with those of the Patrician. This is the front seat of a 1952 model.

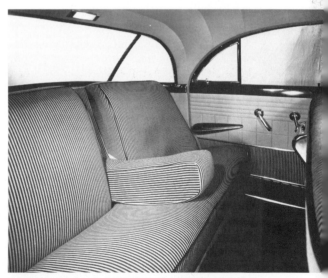

Rear seat area of a 1952 300. Plebian furnishings and four-door body style have rendered the 300 and Cavaliers as overlooked Packards.

wheel openings, rocker panels and trailing lower edges of front fenders, which have built-in salt traps. Chrome was not good in 1952–1953 owing to Korean War shortages, and tends to pit easily; rechroming is expensive and it is easy to spend more restoring one of these models than the restored car will be worth. Upholstery is almost impossible to replicate exactly. The traditional recommendation of buying the best example you can find applies particularly to the 300 and Cavalier.

Identification

1951: Packard name on hood, upswept wings on mascot, chrome strip along rear fender, chrome fin splitting the taillight; lacked chrome gravel deflectors, as found on Patrician.

1952: Packard name dropped from hood, swept-back wings on mascot, chrome molding running across rear fenders and doors, lacked gravel deflectors and fender ornaments, as found on Patrician.

1953: Lowered wings on mascot, no gravel guards, Packard spelled out on rear fenders.

1954: Same as 1953, model identification on trunk lid.

Motor Numbers
1951: J400001–J425000
1952: K400001–K424420
1953: L400001–L418552
1954: M400001–M402638

Production

	1951	1952	1953	1954
Cars	15,309	6,705	10,799	2,580
Bare chassis	401	320	166	205

Specifications

Year	Bore x Stroke	CI	Bhp	Wheelbase
1951–1952 Manual	3.50 x 4.25 in.	327	150	127 in.
1951–1952 Ultramatic	3.50 x 4.25	327	155	127
1953	3.50 x 4.25	327	180	127
1954	3.50 x 4.25	327	185	127

Chassis and drivetrain: Pressed steel I-beam with X-member, independent front suspension, live rear axle with semi-elliptic multiple leaf springs, tubular shocks. Curb weight 3,875 lb. in 1951, 3,380 lb. in 1952, 3,975 lb. in 1953, 3,955 lb. in 1954.

Bodies: Four-door sedan.

Price History

95+ point condition 1	1982	1987	1992	Return
All	$4,300	$7,500	$9,500	17.2%

Chapter 21

Senior Models, 1951–1954

1951–1954 Patrician 400, 1953–1954 Derham Formal Sedan, 1953–1954 Corporation Limousine and 1953–1954 Executive Sedan

	Fun	Investment	Anguish
Patrician 400	4	5	2
Derham Formal Sedan	5	7	3
Executive Sedan	6	7	2
Corporation Limousine	6	8	2

The only all-out luxury car in the Packard lineup for 1951 was the Patrician, riding a wheelbase longer than that of Cadillac's Sixty-two (but not longer than that of the Sixty Special) and with almost as much horsepower (but no V–8). The Patrician cost about $150 more than the Sixty-two, which was no problem, but the breadwinner Cadillac was backed up with a hardtop and con-

vertible. Packard sold 9,000 Patricians in 1951; Cadillac sold 55,000 Sixty-two four-door sedans. It was typical of the unequal contest Packard had been waging with its long-time rival since the late 1940s.

The Patrician carried the suffix 400 and those numbers in gold on the rear roof quarters into 1953. It was an excellent car, beau-

An elegant black 1951 Patrician 400 formerly owned by Don Rook, had under 20,000 miles on the odometer when photographed in 1976. Note cloisonné badges on wheel covers, making their last appearance as they were dropped during the model run.

The Patrician for 1952 gained an extra "bottle opener" on the rear door and the revised hood mascot, but was otherwise similar to the 1951 model. Power brakes became standard and hubcap centers were no longer cloisonné.

tifully built with the best materials, and capable of delivering tireless performance, comfort and luxury over many miles and many years. It has long been a favorite among Packard collectors, and there are probably more Patricians in collector hands today than there are Cadillac Sixty-two sedans—which is revenge of a sort.

The Patrician carried Packard's best engine, the 327 with nine main bearings. Displacement increased to 359 ci in 1954, becoming in the process the most powerful production straight eight ever made. It was a splendid engine, smooth, quiet and potent, but the public wanted V-8s and it cost Packard both image and sales.

A V-8 would have been available much sooner had management opted to spend the money, but in 1953-1954, other things seemed more important: the need to separate Packard from Clipper, the move to a new factory, the Studebaker purchase. The Patrician thus had to make do, and though it had been coaxed up to 212 hp by 1954, Cadillac and Imperial had more power—and more sales potential. After a difficult year in 1954, the Patrician came back fully equipped with snazzy new styling and the essential V-8 (as will be discussed in Chapter 24).

Exterior changes were in detail only for 1952, but fashion designer Dorothy Draper was hired to spruce up interiors and helped develop fine fabrics that were carefully color keyed to the outside paint scheme. Mechanically, Packard introduced Bendix power

Portions of the 1952 Patrician's deluxe duo-tone upholstery are visible in this photo. Traditional interior features during this period were the right-angle shifter knob, flat steering column and heavy metal dash with chrome speaker grille.

This photo of the 1953 Patrician is actually an airbrush job on a 1952. Instantly identifying the 1953 models was the full-length chrome mold-ing with upsweep on front fenders, Packard script on rear fenders and fluted center grille bar.

brakes, a vacuum-assisted system Bendix called Treadlvac and Packard named Easa-matic. The following year Packard added power steering to the Patrician's equipment and brought back the option of air condition-ing, which it had pioneered in 1940.

An interesting 1953 variation was the Derham Formal Sedan, custom-built—or

The 1953 Corporation Limousine built for Pres-ident Eisenhower had air conditioning; note the scoop atop the rear fender. Production of these, and of the similar Derham Formal with padded top and oval backlight, was extremely limited.

Three different back seat treatments were used on 1953–1954 Corporation Limousines. Almost anything could be ordered back here so no hard-and-fast authenticity rule exists, except that upholstery combinations must follow the correct pattern for the individual year.

more accurately custom-finished—by the Philadelphia coachbuilders, whose main contribution was a black padded top with blind rear quarters and a small oval rear window.

What really made the industry take notice was President James Nance's declaration that Packard was out to regain its place as the American standard luxury car. One way to do it, Nance thought, was to get back into the limousine business. Accordingly, for 1953, Packard added a long-wheelbase Executive Sedan and Corporation Limousine, built by Henney and priced respectively at $6,900 and $7,100, to the top of the line.

Much to Nance's disappointment, the long cars failed to put even a small dent in the market for which they were intended. Too much time had gone by, and buyer loyalties were permanently skewed. Cadillac's Seventy-five retained its stranglehold on commercial sales.

What To Look For

Only twenty-five Derhams were built from completed Patrician sedans, so these are the prize models among cars in this group. The limousines and long sedans are next in the hierarchy. They may contain many interior variations, mostly involving the center consoles: Henney would gladly install desks, clocks, liquor cabinets or what-

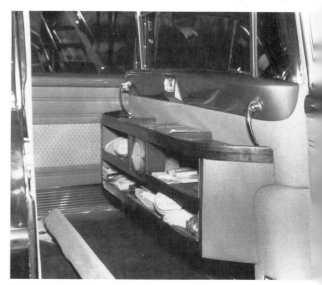

Shelving console on the back partition of another 1953–1954 Corporation Limousine. Formal sedans with padded tops and small rear windows were also available.

Details of the back partition on a 1953–1954 Corporation Limousine.

The showroom at Packard-Detroit in 1954 included, center left, a Corporation Limousine and, center right, a Patrician. Note the shift of the bodyside upsweep to the rear door on these 1954 models. Clippers are in foreground and background.

ever, so no standard applies to interior equipment.

Air conditioning is the most desirable option on 1953–1954 models. Power steering and power brakes were standard on Patricians. The early 1951s were equipped with beautiful cloisonné wheel cover badges of the type previously used on the Custom Eight; these were eventually phased out, but owners of 1951s strive to find a set for their cars.

Problem Areas

Mechanically indestructible, Patricians easily rusted in the salty climates. The worst areas for rust on this body style are above the rear wheel opening, along the rocker panels, behind the rear wheel opening and along the trailing lower edges of the front fenders. The fenders were built by Briggs with multiple layers for strength, but instead of strength they achieved salt-collecting pockets.

Chrome brightwork in 1952–1953 was done without nickel content because of Korean War shortages. The pot-metal parts, specifically including the grille, pitted early in normal outdoor use. The grille, which at the time was the largest die casting in the industry, will cost hundreds to replace or to buy as new-old-stock.

Upholstery, if worn, will be impossible to match exactly. However, the Matelasse-type upholstery of 1954 is normally impervious to anything one can throw at it, and the beautiful broadcloth of other Patricians can be closely approximated by aftermarket suppliers. Patrician headliners were of high-quality material and should be in excellent condition; they can be brushed and vacuumed to remove dirt.

The late 1954 models have an interim-version Ultramatic transmission called Gear-Start Ultramatic, which usually gives trouble and must be overhauled to 1956 standards. See also comments on Ultramatic in Chapter 17.

If the car has hydraulic windows, see also the remarks on this subject in the Problem Areas section of Chapter 16.

Identification

1951: Chrome gravel deflectors, tailfins and fender guards; three ornaments on rear fenders, upswept wings on hood mascot.

1952: Gravel deflectors, four ornaments on rear fenders, sweptback wings on hood mascot.

1953: Gravel deflectors, lowered wings on hood mascot, full-length bodyside molding with kick-up on front fender; Derham Formal Sedan had padded top with small backlight and Derham script on fender; Corporation Limousine had division window and auxiliary seats; Executive Sedan had auxiliary seats.

1954: Same as 1953 with bodyside molding kick-up now on rear door; backup lamps incorporated in taillight housings, peaked headlamp rims.

Production

Model	1951	1952	1953	1954
Patrician sedan	9,001	3,975	7,456	2,760
Derham Formal Sedan	—	—	25	—
Corporation Limousine	—	—	50	35
Executive sedan	—	—	100	65

Specifications

Year	Bore x Stroke	CI	Bhp	Wheelbase
1951–1952	3.50 x 4.25 in.	327	155	127 in.
1953	3.50 x 4.25	327	180	127, 149
1954	3.56 x 4.25	359	212	127, 149

Chassis and drivetrain: Pressed steel I-beam with X-member, independent front suspension, live rear axle with semi-elliptic multiple leaf springs, tubular shocks. Curb weight: 4,200 lb. on Patrician, 4,335 lb. on Derham, 4,650 lb. on Executive Sedan, 4,720 lb. on Corporation Limousine.

Bodies: Four-door sedan in all years. Formal sedan in 1953. Long-wheelbase sedan and limousine in 1953–1954.

Price History

95+ point condition 1	1982	1987	1992	Return
Patrician	$6,000	$ 9,000	$12,000	14.9%
Derham formal sedan	7,500	12,000	18,000	19.1
Executive Sedan	6,500	10,000	14,000	16.6
Corporate Limousine	7,000	11,000	16,000	18.0

Motor Numbers

1951: J600001–J610000
1952: K400001–K424420
1953: L600001–L607829
1954: M600001–M605618

Chapter 22

Caribbean, 1953–1954

Models 2678 and 5478

	Fun	Investment	Anguish
Caribbean	9	9	5

The Caribbean, Packard's flagship of the 1950s, was designed by a young stylist named Dick Teague, who applied some of the ideas from the Henney Company's experimental Pan American to a conventional 250 convertible, gave it a hood scoop, a continental spare and a flashy interior, and added chrome wire wheels with full wheel cutouts to show them off. The result was a "sports car" Packard happily offered the public at a mere $5,200.

Unfortunately, production delays held shipments back until March. To build Caribbeans, Packard decided to ship standard 1953 convertibles to Mitchell-Bentley, a specialty manufacturer in Ionia, Michigan, which did the finish work. This took more time than the Sales Department had counted on, but most major dealerships had a Caribbean on the floor by spring. Curiously, Packard did not use the senior 327 with nine main bearings on the 1953 Caribbean, but in 1954, when that engine was enlarged to 359 ci, it did use this powerplant. (See "Salon: 1953 Caribbean," by Burt Weaver, in *The Packard Cormorant*, number 21; and "Salon: 1954 Caribbean," by Michael Richards, in *The Packard Cormorant*, number 26.)

The Caribbean was a bargain compared with Cadillac's $7,750 Eldorado, though a

The beautiful Caribbean in its first year, 1953. With the cleanest styling of all four years, the 1953 is also the highest-production Caribbean, though collectors tend to prefer the 1955–1956 models. Full wheel cutouts were unique to the model.

Backup lamps on 1953 Caribbeans were separately mounted under taillamps; compare this to the integral treatment of the 1954s.

much closer competitor was the Buick Skylark, also $5,200. For once Packard triumphed over Cadillac, selling 750 Caribbeans to only 400 Eldorados. Such figures are unimportant in the larger scheme of things, but no doubt the Caribbean did a lot for Packard at a time when its image needed a lift and was welcomed by dealers as a showroom traffic booster. Nowadays it boosts traffic at Packard meets. No other model of its era is desired more by Packard collectors.

A stand-fast policy in 1954, putting off a complete restyle and new engineering until 1955, implied little change for the Caribbean. Plans for a hardtop version were shelved, a few small engineering and design changes were made, and the price was raised to $6,100. Despite two-thirds fewer sales overall in 1954 compared with 1953, Packard still managed to unload 400 Caribbeans. But rival Eldorado—now less customized and drastically cut in price—sold 2,150, and kept on going in the years ahead. By 1956, the Eldorado was making money, while the Caribbean had become just an expensive albatross around the corporate neck. (See Chapter 25.)

The most distinguishing 1954 feature was a two-tone color panel running down from the rear of the doors and back across the rear fender tops and deck. A new dashboard, unique to this model year, and lowered rear wheel cutouts were the other obvious changes; under the hood was the nine-main Patrician engine, an important upgrade from 1953. Power windows and seats, a radio and a heater were all standard.

What To Look For

Collectors have noticed many detail differences among early 1953 models compared with the later versions. For instance, Packard script appeared on the front quarter panels of early cars, just behind the wheel openings, but was not present on later examples. The first car (2678–1001) and probably a few that followed had a chrome-plated trim piece on the leading edge of the hood scoop. Other detail changes probably occurred as production progressed. Manual transmission was technically available, but almost all cars came with Ultramatic.

A magnificent example of the breed is Joe Jankovic's red and white 1954 Caribbean from Chicago. *Bud Juneau*

Rear view of the 1954 Caribbean in red and white two-toning. The two-tone pattern was standard and unique to the model. *Bud Juneau*

Dashboard and cockpit of the 1954 Caribbean. *Bud Juneau*

Rear wheel cutouts were lowered on the 1954 Caribbean. *Bud Juneau*

The 1954 model is the rarest among the four years of Caribbean production but has not developed much of a lead over the 1953 in market price and continues to cost less, car for car, than the 1955–1956 models. These considerations make the 1954 a best buy, as sooner or later its scarcity will cause it to rise more rapidly in value.

Problem Areas

Mechanically, and from the standpoint of rust, Caribbeans are similar to Patricians of the same years (see Chapter 21). But Caribbeans are actually easier to restore, since the upholstery is leather—no stamped patterns, just straight off the cow and dyed. Certain die-cast parts unique to Caribbeans, around the wheel openings and along the side, present supply difficulties.

The wire wheels that were standard on these cars deserve a close look. The slightest

peeling and rusting will require replacement or overhaul for show. Modern fit-ups are available but are not identical.

Production

Model	1953	1954
All	750	400

Identification

1953: Unique hood with wide air scoop and no hood mascot, fully radiused rear wheel cutouts, chrome wire wheels.

1954: Chrome molding running down from rear of doors straight back along fenders, usually a two-tone demarcation line; peaked headlamp rims; backup lights incorporated in taillight assembly.

Motor Numbers

1953: L400001–L418552
1954: M600001–M605618

Specifications

Year	Bore x Stroke	CI	Bhp	Wheelbase
1953	3.50 x 4.25 in.	327	180	122 in.
1954	3.56 x 4.25	359	212	122

Chassis and drivetrain: Pressed steel I-beam frame with X-member, independent front suspension, live rear axle with semi-elliptic multiple leaf springs, tubular shocks.

Curb weight 4,265 lb. in 1953, 4,660 lb. in 1954.

Bodies: Two-door convertible.

Price History

95+ point condition 1	1982	1987	1992	Return
1953	$11,000	$21,000	$32,000	22.2%
1954	13,000	22,000	35,000	20.5

Chapter 23

Junior Models, 1955–1956

1955 Packard Clipper, 1956 Clipper and 1956 Executive

	Fun	Investment	Anguish
Executive hardtop	6	6	7
Clipper hardtop	6	5	7
Executive sedan	3	4	7
Clipper sedans	3	3	7

Had things turned out differently, the Clipper game plan for 1955–1956 would be hailed today as a brilliant solution to Packard's schizoid post-World War II image: separating the Packard marque from the medium-priced cars and building a separate identity for the latter. That's just what James Nance set out to do, and he achieved it in 1956, formally registering Clipper as a separate make in its own right—to the howls of the dealers, who hadn't gotten the message and were still selling it as a Packard. As Nance told me, "You couldn't blame them—they wanted something to sell." But by 1956, for reasons that had little to do with its actual products, Packard was on the ropes.

Packard purchased Studebaker in 1954, and with it a failing enterprise that required some 200,000 cars or more in annual volume just to break even—a level Studebaker hadn't attained since 1951. Packard itself, now a division of Studebaker-Packard, made a tactical error: faced with the loss of its Briggs-built bodies after Briggs sold out to Chrysler in 1954, Nance and Company bought a new, smaller plant on Connor Avenue in Detroit and transferred much of the Packard assembly there.

It was thought that the one-story Connor plant would be more efficient, and probably in the long run it would have been, but the problems of starting there from scratch were immense and numerous quality complaints were made. This occurred at precisely the wrong time, since 1955 was a banner year for car sales, and a Packard without such problems undoubtedly would have done much better. The upshot was that Packard Division sold only about 55,000 1955s, including 38,000 Clippers, and some 29,000 of its 1956s, including 18,000 Clippers.

The Clipper was limited competitively because it offered only two body styles—four-door sedan and hardtop—since the Connor plant could not be tooled for any more. That meant axing the two-door sedans and being unable to add a station wagon or a four-door hardtop. The 1955 Packard Clipper did offer three trim levels (Deluxe, Super, Custom) embracing a trio of sedans and two hardtops. The hardtops comprised the low-end Super Panama at $2,776 base price and the flashy Custom Constellation at $3,076 base price.

In 1956, Packard Division produced an upmarket model called the Packard Executive—a kind of cross between Clipper and Packard—plus Clippers in the five previous models and body styles. The latter were now registered as Clipper automobiles.

All Clippers and the Executive featured Packard's innovative Torsion-Level suspension, although a conventional suspension was available on the bottom-line Deluxe. The invention of Bill Allison, who had spent years and money trying to peddle it to other Detroit companies before he came to Packard, Torsion-Level suspension was an interlinked torsion-bar arrangement operating on all four wheels. A complicated electrical system allowed the suspension to correct for load weight, and the interlinking of all four wheels provided truly extraordinary ride and handling. An impressive film shows a 1955 Patrician and Cadillac driving over the same Detroit railroad crossing at the same high rate of speed: the Cadillac appears to have lost contact with its back axle, whereas the Packard seems to have passed a small undulation in the road.

The initial design for the 1955 Clipper called for a two-tone pattern to cover roof, deck and upper rear fuselage, as on this Custom sedan. After Packard had a look at the 1955 Pontiac, however, another two-tone section was added along the lower front fenders and doors, giving a kind of candy-cane effect to the more brightly painted examples, as on this 1955 Constellation hardtop. *Eastern Packard Club*

Many think a one-tone Clipper is an altogether better-looking car, but monotones were not popular in 1955 and most of the cars are in two-color. This handsome Custom from Pennsylvania is pulling into a Packard Club national meet.

More important, a powerful new over-square V–8 was under the hood of each car, and the Ultramatic was improved to deal with the higher torque of the V–8. In 1956, Ultramatic cars had a unique pushbutton control panel, sprouting from a heavy arm under the steering wheel. The 1956s were mildly facelifted, especially at the rear, where they had rakishly pointed taillights,

Bare bones for 1956 was the Model 5622 Clipper Deluxe four-door sedan. This perfect example is owned by Ian Avery of Winstead, Connecticut. *Eastern Packard Club*

which were also used on the Packard Executive.

What To Look For

The Executive hardtop, production barely 1,000, is the scarcest and most desirable junior Packard of this period. Clipper hardtops had much higher volume. Among these, the Custom Constellation is preferable to the Super Panama. The 1956 Constellation saw fewer than 1,500 units and is scarce. Little or no interest is shown in the sedans, and these should be passed up unless they are in very fine original or restored condition.

Though Ultramatic was an option on Clippers, it was almost always ordered; a manual shift example would be an interesting find. On the other hand, low-line DeLuxe Clippers with conventional suspensions offer little of technical interest.

The Deluxe and Super sedans have lately caught the Custom in value, but this is probably because they're all relatively the same, and just an instance of market corrections. The best investments are clearly the hardtops, the Executive in particular.

Problem Areas

The 1955 Packards and Clippers had more gadgets than any previous models and provide many opportunities for things to break. Twin Ultramatic transmission in 1955 was taxed by powerful V–8 engines and is best

The 1956 Executive, a kind of a cross between the Clipper and Packard, was created to fill a perceived market gap. It had Clipper taillights but the ornate Packard grille and, usually, a full-width two-tone panel along the body side.

Factory artwork of the 1956 Clipper Custom sedan, the most elaborately trimmed Clipper, shows the handsome taillights that distinguish the 1956 from the 1955. They were later used on Studebaker-based Packards during 1957 and 1958.

brought up to 1956 standards during any overhaul. Check for a direct clutch that does not engage or slips (groans) under load: engine flare or runaway between first and second in the D-range; or burned transmission fluid. (See also other Ultramatic comments in Chapter 17.)

Rod bearings in V–8 engines need attention well before 100,000 miles or crankshaft damage may result.

Check all the "fifties gadgets": power steering, power seats, power brakes, power antennas, signal-seeking radio, power windows, air conditioning and, on 1956 models, the electric pushbutton transmission shifter.

Be sure the leveler on the Torsion-Level suspension operates properly. If torsion bars are sagged out and no further adjustment is possible through the replaceable load link, you will find that replacement torsion bars are difficult to get.

Production

Model	1955	1956
Deluxe sedan	8,039	5,715
Super sedan	7,979	5,173
Super Panama hardtop	7,016	3,999

The 1956 Clipper Super hardtop, a cleanly styled car, shows how hard Studebaker-Packard was working to establish a separate marque image for the Clipper: helmwheels on the hubs, rear roof pillars and grille, Clipper script across the hood and a distinctive hood ornament.

Custom sedan	8,708	2,129
Custom Constellation hardtop	6,672	1,466
Executive sedan	—	1,784
Executive hardtop	—	1,031

Identification

1955: Vertical-bar grille, 1954 style taillights with backup light incorporated underneath, Clipper script on hood. Series identification on trunk lid: Deluxe had conventional suspension, fabric upholstery; Super had leather-trimmed upholstery; Custom had leather-trimmed upholstery and rear seat armrests. Two-toning began on hood, swept downward along doors and ran back along lower rear fenders.

1956: Horizontal-bar grille, new slipper-shaped taillights with sharp points at tops. Model differences as listed for 1955. Two-tone panels ran straight along body sides.

Specifications

Year	Model	Bore x Stroke	CI	Bhp	Wheelbase
1955	Deluxe and Super	3.81 x 3.50 in.	320	225	122 in.
1955	Custom	4.00 x 3.50	352	245	122
1956	Deluxe and Super	4.00 x 3.50	352	240	122
1956	Custom	4.00 x 3.50	352	275	122
1956	Packard Executive	4.00 x 3.50	352	275	122

Chassis and drivetrain: Pressed steel I-beam frame with X-member, independent front suspension, live rear axle.

1955–1956 Deluxe and 1955 Super: Semi-elliptic multiple leaf rear springs, tubular shocks.

1956 Super, 1955–1956 Custom, 1956 Packard Executive, and optional on Deluxe and Super from mid–1955: Packard full-length torsion bar suspension with automatic load compensator.

Curb weight: From 3,670 lb. on 1955 Super sedan to 4,185 lb. on 1956 Packard Executive hardtop.

Serial Numbers

1955 Deluxe sedan: 5522–1001 to 5522–9039

1955 Super sedan: 5542–1001 to 5542–8979

1955 Super Panama hardtop: 5547–1001 to 5547–8016

1955 Custom sedan: 5562–1001 to 5562–9708

1955 Custom Constellation hardtop: 5567–1001 to 5567–7672

1956 Deluxe sedan: 5622–1001 to 5622–6715

1956 Super sedan: 5642–1001 to 5642–6173

1956 Super Panama hardtop: 5647–1001 to 5647–4999

1956 Custom sedan: 5662–1001 to 5662–3129

1956 Custom Constellation hardtop: 5667–1001 to 5667–2466

1956 Executive sedan: 5672–1001 to 5672–2784

1956 Executive hardtop: 5677–1001 to 5677–2031

Price History

95+ point condition 1	1982	1987	1992	Return
Deluxe and Super sedans	$3,200	$6,500	$7,500	18.6%
Custom and Executive sedans	4,500	7,000	8,000	12.2
Super Panama hardtop	4,000	7,500	10,000	20.1
Custom Constellation hardtop	4,500	8,000	11,500	20.6
Executive hardtop	4,500	7,500	13,000	23.6

Chapter 24

Senior Models, 1955–1956

Patrician and Four Hundred

	Fun	Investment	Anguish
Patrician sedan	5	6	5
Four Hundred hardtop	6	7	5

Despite its corporate and financial woes, Packard built some of its most brilliant cars in 1955–1956, and these top-of-the-line models are popular among today's collectors. Small wonder, since they were manifestly state-of-the-art, and ahead-of-the-art in certain ways, particularly with regard to their Torsion-Level suspension system. (The background to this remarkable innovation was discussed in Chapter 23.)

Equally important in 1955, old straight-eight engines had finally been replaced by modern overhead-valve V–8s. Packard put its largest V–8s into its senior models, the four-door sedan Patrician and the two-door hardtop Four Hundred.

A clever facelift of the old bodies and the long-needed stretch of the hardtop to the 127 in. wheelbase gave Packard up-to-date mid-1950s styling: wraparound windshield, "cathedral" taillights, exhaust ducts out the back bumpers, vivid two-tone paint jobs interrupted by fancy brightmetal trim, be-jeweled dashboard, and flashy interiors of cloth and leather.

In bringing the hardtop model name Four Hundred, Packard was invoking New York's "social four hundred" families, an appropriately snooty monicker. The Patrician name had been around since 1951, and as names go was pretty good. Alas, the company never got around to producing long-wheelbase models, much to the displeasure of President Nance, who thought Packard was abandoning an important image by not making any—and he was right.

Although sales were reasonably good in 1955, orders for the mildly facelifted 1956s plummeted, partly because of public doubt over the viability of Studebaker-Packard, partly because of quality and service problems on the 1955s. Ironically, the 1956s were well built, with most of the early bugs eliminated. Ultramatic had a new electronic con-

Cleverly facelifted by Dick Teague and Bill Schmidt on a now-aging body shell, the 1955 Patrician looked as up-to-date as any competitor. Restorations of this glitzy Packard are costly, as you might gather from that dental work.

The Four Hundred was Packard's hardtop counterpart to the Patrician in 1955. Note the practical outside courtesy lamp built into the leading edge of the rear fender. "Reynolds Wrap" side trim extends only halfway back on 1955 models.

What To Look For

The odd monotone Patrician or Four Hundred looks much better today than the two-tone jobs, but these cars are hard to find unless you repaint one that way, which will cost points if the judges know how to interpret paint codes. Model for model the 1956s are rarer than the 1955s, and less inclined to cause trouble. All of these cars appreciated strongly during the 1980s, the Patrician an impressive value gainer among postwar production sedans. By the 1990s, Four Hundreds commanded prices that were paid for convertible models of contemporary Cadillacs, Lincolns and Imperials.

Problem Areas

The 1955–1956 Patrician and Four Hundred had more gadgets than any previous models, and therefore more opportunities for things to break. The Twin Ultramatic transmission of 1955 was taxed to the limit by the powerful V–8 engines and upon any major overhaul is best brought up to 1956 standards. Check for a direct clutch that does not engage or slips (groans) under load; engine flare or runaway between first and second in D-range; or burned transmission fluid (see also other Ultramatic comments in Chapter 17).

trol and horsepower was up. It made no difference.

Nance, after failing to obtain loans for an all-new line of 1957 Packards, turned over management of Studebaker-Packard to the Curtiss-Wright Corporation. He stayed on the job long enough to get some of his top managers placed elsewhere around Detroit, and then left . . . to head up the Edsel Division. Later in life Nance told me that he finally got into the banking business "because you can't do anything without money."

The 1956 Patrician had peaked headlamp rims—which are terrific rust-catchers—and full-width "Reynolds Wrap" along the body to distinguish it from the 1955. Interiors were the most deluxe available.

The rod bearings in the V–8 engines need attention well before 100,000 miles or crankshaft damage may result.

Check all the "fifties gadgets": power steering, power seats, power brakes, power antennas, signal-seeking radio, power windows, air conditioning and, on 1956s only, the electric pushbutton transmission shifter.

Find out if the leveler on the Torsion-Level suspension operates properly. If for some reason the torsion bars in the suspension are sagged out and no more adjustment can be had through the replaceable load link, you will find replacement torsion bars difficult to get.

Production

Model	1955	1956
Patrician sedan	9,127	3,775
Four Hundred hardtop	7,206	3,224

Identification

1955: Shallow peaks over headlamps, grille formed by horizontal and vertical bars extending width of car, model identification on front fenders in gold script, 1954-style Packard crest built around keyhole on deck.

1956: Deep, pointed peaks over headlamps, grille has mesh background, V and circle grille emblem repeated on deck.

Specifications

Engines:

1955: Overhead-valve V–8, 352 ci (4.00 x 3.50 in.), 260 bhp.

1956: Overhead-valve V–8, 374 ci (4.13 x 3.50 in.), 290 bhp.

Wheelbase: 127 in.

Chassis and drivetrain: Pressed steel I-beam frame with X-member, independent front suspension, live rear axle, Packard full-length torsion-bar suspension with automatic load compensator. Curb weight: 4,275 lb. on 1955 Patrician, 4,045 lb. on 1956 Patrician, 4,250 lb. on 1955 Four Hundred, 4,080 lb. on 1956 Four Hundred.

Serial Numbers

1955 Patrician: 5582–1001 to 5582–10127

1955 Four Hundred: 5587–1001 to 5587–8206

1956 Patrician: 5682–1001 to 5682–4775

1956 Four Hundred: 5687–1001 to 5687–4224

Price History

95+ point condition 1	1982	1987	1992	Return
Patrician	$4,500	$10,000	$13,000	23.6%
Four Hundred	6,000	14,000	20,000	27.2

The Four Hundred hardtop, virtually always two-toned, is one of the most popular Packards among collectors today, and considering its relatively low production, many survived. Peaked headlamps identify the 1956 version.

Chapter 25

Caribbean, 1955–1956

Models 5580, 5697 and 5699

	Fun	Investment	Anguish
Convertible	9	10	7
Hardtop	6	8	7

Combining all the engineering breakthroughs of 1955 with the exclusivity of a limited-production car, the third-generation Packard Caribbean was the most luxurious and extroverted to date, and the first to ride the 127 in. wheelbase. The wheelbase change was achieved, as on the 1955 Four Hundred hardtop, by a clever new technique

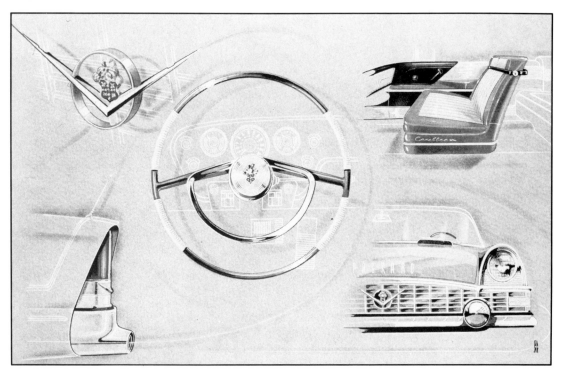

Factory art showed design details of the 1955 Caribbean. With the new circle-and-vee motif, stylist Dick Teague told me, "I was trying to create a design as simple and timeless as the Mercedes-Benz star." Packard didn't have enough time left.

involving plastic tooling, which was 60 percent less expensive than conventional metal tools and also a lot quicker to fabricate.

To the 1955 bonuses of Torsion-Level suspension, a big V–8 engine and revised Ultramatic with low-range takeoff, Packard added as standard equipment every available option except air conditioning, wire wheels and tinted or shaded glass. For good measure the 352 ci V–8 was modified with twin Rochester carburetors, which helped it develop 275 bhp, 15 bhp more than the 1955 Patrician and—probably not quite by accident—5 bhp more than the Cadillac Eldorado. In fact, aside from the Chrysler 300, the 1955 Caribbean was the most powerful production car in America that year.

Exclusive styling remained a hallmark of the Caribbean in 1955. The new model had a special hood with double louvers, a continuous midbody stripe from front to rear, and three-tone paint jobs, the last item shared only with Dodge and DeSoto.

Curiously, though, considering what it had to offer and the number dealers said they could have sold, management decided to build only 500 Caribbeans for the model year. The reason seems to be that exclusive-to-Caribbean items, like the special hood, had been run off in advance to a limit of 500 plus enough to stock for spare parts, and the accountants said it would be uneconomical to produce another smallish run for the sake of a few more sales. They weren't watching Cadillac, which had by now determined to make money with the rival Eldorado and built nearly 4,000 units in 1955. Today a 1955 Caribbean is worth more than a 1955 Eldorado, but six years after the two models were introduced the Caribbean had a retail value of $435 while the Cadillac stood at $1,138. (See "Three-toned Luxury: The 1955 Caribbean," by George L. Hamlin, in *The Packard Cormorant*, number 38.)

Barely more Caribbeans were built in 1956, a year when Packard generally took a sales beating—indeed the Caribbean was the only Packard or Clipper to see more production in 1956 than it did in 1955. Had the public not begun to doubt that Packard wasn't long for this world, they probably would have bought a lot more Caribbeans,

As long as a yacht with all the features that turned folks on in 1955—three-tone paint, dual antennas, dual exhausts, a jewellike dash and cathedral taillights—the Caribbean continues to fascinate many collectors today.

because the 1956 was an even grander product. Offered now as a hardtop as well as a convertible, the three-toned flagship of the line had a revised grille and fenders and other detail changes, and the center body stripe.

Engineering changes for 1956 included pushbutton Twin Ultramatic transmission, Twin Traction differential, negative-ground electrical system, improved Torsion-Level suspension and a displacement increase to 374 ci. Again, the Caribbean had a horsepower edge on the Patrician and Four Hundred. At 310 bhp, the Caribbean still paced the new Eldorado engine by 5 bhp.

Except for the Chrysler 300's Hemi, the Caribbean V–8 engine was the most powerful in the industry.

An uncommon two-tone 1955 Caribbean owned by Fred and Dan Kanter of New Jersey, with what I think are dubious wire wheel covers—but Kanter Brothers is a chief supplier of Packard parts, so perhaps these are some weird dealer permutation. The Caribbean looked stunning in two-tone. *Eastern Packard Club*

The way manufacturers lied about their gross horsepower in those days, however, only a dynamometer could tell which car was really more powerful.

At just short of $6,000, and $500 less for the hardtop, the Caribbean was an expensive car, but not nearly as expensive as the Cadillac Eldorado, which had also expanded with a hardtop in 1956. Both open and closed Eldorados started at around $6,600, yet they sold 6,000 units while Packard flogged only 539 Caribbeans. Once again, Packard's short count was owed partly to the decision to build only about 500 and partly to lack of Packard buyers with that kind of money. By

1956, everybody expected the nameplate to disappear, which was poison to a car's reputation in the 1950s—nobody wanted an orphan.

Studebaker-Packard Corporation ran into financial disaster when the banks and other investors who would normally have funded much of its development backed away in 1956, forcing the resignation of Nance and a takeover by Curtiss-Wright, which was buying mainly for tax advantages. Had the company not run into this difficulty, the fifth-generation 1957 Caribbean would have been something. Fully redesigned around the Predictor show car, it would certainly have offered over 400 ci of V-8, since the 374 block was said to be expandable to 500 ci, and over 350 bhp. Some thought even existed about a Caribbean V-12.

Corporate woes stopped all this planning in its tracks. Spare parts were used to overbuild by 39 on the planned 500, mostly for special orders; Curtiss-Wright offered a final gratuitous kick by selling off the remaining stock of Caribbean seat cushions for use in boats.

What To Look For

A handful of 1955 Caribbean hardtops are known to exist, but are not factory production models. Rather, they are the work of dealerships or even private owners, who converted Four Hundreds to Caribbean specs on their own.

New for 1956, and unique among all four years, was the Caribbean hardtop. The Hypalon top covering tended to leak and induce rust in the place you're least likely to look for it: the roof. *Eastern Packard Club*

Among 1956 models, grilles exist with bold chrome and anodized gold backing mesh, the latter a running change made after Packard saw the 1956 Cadillacs; gold is preferred among collectors.

A novel feature of the 1956 was its reversible seat cushions: multicolor boucle fabric on one side, pleated leather on the other. These seats weren't foolproof: They fall forward on even moderate braking, and a factory kit to fix this is rarely found working anymore. At the time, they cost far more than they were worth. But they do offer something nobody else has ever offered in a car—spare upholstery! Be sure you look on both sides when you examine a car for purchase.

The production tickets on almost all the 1956 Caribbeans were preserved by former Studebaker-Packard employee Roscoe Stelford, and a roster of 1955–1956 Caribbeans is expertly maintained by Stuart R. Blond (see Parts and Services section at the end of this book). Prospective buyers should write to Blond for background information on these Caribbeans and also to learn exactly how they were originally painted and trimmed. This will help divulge any alterations in any specific car from its original condition. (For a detailed rundown of the many variations, refer to "All the 1956 Caribbeans," by Stuart R. Blond, in *The Packard Cormorant*, number 48.)

Research like Stelford's and Blond's is important because many 1956 variations existed, especially toward the end, when Packard was building to order. For example, while more than 200 convertibles used one of the four standard three-tone color combinations, 31 had monotone paint jobs, 25 had two-tones and 12 had paint jobs remain unknown or may have left the factory "in the white." Likewise, although four standard interior combinations were offered, many special-order interiors were produced, of which Blond has identified six (see Specifications section below).

Problem Areas

Every comment about their stablemates, Patrician and Four Hundred (see this section in Chapter 24) applies to Caribbeans, only more so—because, while twin rear antennas, pushbutton transmission shifters and so on were options on the other cars, all these toys were standard on the Caribbeans. Check them for proper working condition. The convertible models want the usual attention to the top, but hardtops warrant a warning all their own.

Packard used white Hypalon vinyl for the 1956 hardtop roof cover. The result looked impressive but Hypalon turned out to be semipermeable. Water could and did get under it, usually through the longitudinal seams, and once in it had no place to go. Rusted roofs were the peculiar malady that this caused, and anyone investigating a 1956 Caribbean should first check for rust and second be sure the material, if replaced, is a close match to the original.

Production

Model	1955	1956
Convertible	500	276
Hardtop	—	263

Identification

1955: Three-tone paint job standard (but one- and two-tone patterns exist), shallow peaked headlamps, hood with two scoops but no ornament and no Packard crest, 1954-style deck handle with crest and keyhole.

1956: Mesh backing behind grille and parking lights with bumper bombs moved outward, deeply hooded front fenders with fender crown removed, reshaped hood with Packard crest added, circle-and-vee trunk handle and revised trunk nameplates, redesigned rear bumper, larger dash clock, redesigned gas tank doorhandle.

Serial Numbers

1955: 5588-1001 to 5588-1500

1956 Convertible: 5699-1001B to 5699-1276A

1956 Hardtop: 5697-1001 to 5697-1263

Note: letters following last four digits are believed to indicate status of the order: A for cars delivered as ordered, B for orders canceled and then reordered, C for cars reordered twice, and so on.

Specifications

Year	Bore x Stroke	CI	Bhp	Wheelbase
1955	4.00 x 3.50 in.	352	275	127 in.
1956	4.13 x 3.50	374	310	127

Chassis and drivetrain: Channel side members and X-brace with extra-depth re-inforcement, independent front suspension, live rear axle with torque arms, full-length torsion-bar suspension with automatic load compensator, tubular shocks. Curb weight 4,755 lb. on 1955 convertible, 4,960 lb. on 1956 convertible, 4,590 lb. on 1956 hardtop.

Bodies: Two-door convertible in 1955 and 1956; two-door hardtop in 1956.

1955 Paint combinations: Standard three-tone combinations: MAC, MDF, MJV, MUH. Individual colors available as follows: A=Jade, B=Tourmaline, C=Emerald Metallic, D=Zircon, E=Ultramarine Metallic, F=Sapphire Metallic, G=Moonstone, H=Grey Pearl Metallic, J=Fire Opal, K=Topac Metallic, L=Turquoise, M=White Jade, N=Agate, P=Citrine, R=Sardonyx, U=Rose Quartz and V=Onyx.

1955 Trim combinations: 92=White and Light Blue, 93=White and Light Green, 96=White and Red, 97=White and Fuschia.

1956 Paint combinations: Standard two- and three-tone combinations: EME, EMS, HMH, LLN, MAV, MES, MKC, MKN, MNN, MTM, MTV, NMN, NTN, PPV, VMV, VTV. Individual colors available as follows: A=Shannon Green, B=Tahitian Jade Metallic, C=Eire Green, D=Norwegian Forest Metallic, E=Danube Blue, F=Holland Blue Metallic, G=Aegean Blue Metallic, H=Adriatic Blue Metallic, J=Tangier Red, K=Scottish Heather, L=Persian Aqua, M=Dover White, N=Maltese Gray Metallic, O=Flamingo, P=Jamaican Yellow, R=Mojave Tan Metallic, S=Roman Copper Metallic, T=Naples Orange, V=Corsican Black.

1956 Convertible trim combinations: 90=Vermillion and White leather, Gray cloth; 92=Blue and White leather, Copper cloth; 93=Green and White leather, Gray cloth; 96=Red and White leather, Gray cloth.

1956 Hardtop trim combinations: Same as convertibles, numbered 290, 292, 293 and 296 respectively.

1956 Special interiors known: 37=White leather both sides and on dash padding; 72=Black and White leather; 131=Gray door panels (no other details known); 195=Brown two-tone leather and cloth; 196=Black and White (no other details known); 201=Scottish Heather both sides, gray dashboard.

1956 Convertible variants:

Car 1074 has column shift.

Cars 1009, 1012, 1029 and 1040 have chrome grille mesh, others known have anodized gold mesh.

Car 1021 had factory-installed seatbelts, was built for Earle C. Anthony Inc. and had special ECA hood ornament mounted atop standard one.

Cars 1049, 1084, 1116, 1117, 1167 and 1228 had factory wire wheels, although other cars were retrofitted.

Cars 1019 and 1197, and possibly others, had rear seat speakers.

Car 1208 carries stainless steel ribbed chrome bodyside trim normally found on Patricians and Four Hundreds.

Fifteen cars had factory air conditioning.

1956 Hardtop variants:

Car 1245 was built without the Hypalon vinyl top.

Car 1226 was scrapped, but its data plate was placed on a Four Hundred converted to Caribbean specs. It is likely other such made-over examples exist.

Price History

95+ point condition 1	1982	1987	1992	Return
Convertible	10,000	25,000	35,000	24.6%
Hardtop	9,000	22,500	29,500	25.0

Chapter 26

Packard Clipper, 1957

Town Sedan and Country Sedan

	Fun	Investment	Anguish
Town Sedan	4	3	3
Country Sedan (wagon)	4	5	3

Circumstances conspired to close Packard's historic East Grand Boulevard plant and not-so-historic Connor plant in Detroit after the final 1956 models had been built. To preserve the marque and meet dealer franchise commitments, "Packards," which were in fact restyled senior Studebakers, were built in the Studebaker factory at South Bend, Indiana. The 1957 line, which packed Studebaker's powerful supercharged V–8, consisted of a Town Sedan and Country Sedan, the latter being Packard's first station wagon since 1950. Both were designated Packard Clippers.

To his great credit, stylist Dick Teague was able to transfer many Packard design hallmarks to what was essentially a Studebaker President shell: the traditional-shape radiator grille, the handsome "slipper" taillights of the 1956 Clippers, a dashboard resembling that of 1956, and lots of hexagon and helmwheel emblems. A bodyside molding of beaded brightmetal, the stuff people call "Reynolds Wrap," was even included, thinner but similar to that of the 1956 Patrician and Four Hundred.

The two models sold for about $3,300 base or about $4,000 as typically delivered, well down from previous Packard price levels. But with 275 hp from the supercharged Studebaker 289 ci V–8, they carried the same output as the 1955 Caribbean, and were quicker because of their lighter weight. The engine even carried Packard valve cover

decals. Borg-Warner Flightomatic automatic transmission, Packard Twin Traction differential, Studebaker variable-rate coil springs and variable-ratio steering were also part of the package.

Standard equipment included backup lights, padded dash, clock, carpeting and foam rubber cushions. Power brakes, steering, windows, seats and antennas, as well as air conditioning, were available at extra cost.

Interiors were as luxurious as they could be, given their Studebaker origins, and the

Dick Teague, told to design a Studebaker that looked like a Packard, did his best. He retained the traditional shape of the Packard grille, which dated back to the 1904 Model L, and the helmwheel, which had come along only a few years before to signify the Clipper, as all 1957 Packards were called.

Studebaker parentage is obvious, but you have to hand it to Teague for doing so well with the little he had. Recalling a more noble past were the skinny "Reynolds Wrap" side molding, dual antennas, 1955 hood ornament and Clipper wheel covers.

idea of a well-equipped, supercharged station wagon was unique. Arguably, a hardtop would have been more appealing, but time was short and decisions had to be made. The new 1957 Packards were introduced toward the end of January 1957, after months of speculation over whether a Packard would appear at all. It did, but it proved to be a disappointment: fewer than 5,000 were sold, most of them sedans.

Throwing all the quality available at the 1957 Packard Clipper, Studebaker-Packard tried to maintain the marque until a new, big Packard could reappear. It never did.

What To Look For

Few variations occur among these two models, and little difference in value exists between them if you are to believe the price guides. In fact, however, the wagon was outbuilt four to one by the sedan and retains the status of a rare car—if you accept as rare any production run of under 1,000.

Look also for the optional accessories, especially factory air, power seats and power radio antennas. Primarily, though, be sure that the cars are clean and original.

Problem Areas

Rust—or Studitis, as it is called among collectors—is a commonly known malady whose first effects are evident on front fenders just forward of the doors, where a vertical line of bubbles forms which rapidly evolve to rust. This is the product of a moisture-collecting fender design started in 1947 and never rectified. If you find a rust-free car and want to keep it that way, invest in a thorough rustproofing by an expert, followed by a renewal of weather seals.

The Studebaker drivetrain is reliable. Borg-Warner's automatic is its weakest link, but its repair is not beyond the resourceful transmission mechanic. Brakes are adequate. Rear axles on these relatively high-performance cars should be carefully examined for wear.

The small-block Studebaker V-8 is a notorious oil leaker but not a serious oil burner and is well known for running up large, six-figure mileage without an overhaul. It may not quite match the lightness and horsepower per cubic inch of Chevy's 283, but it tends to last longer and delivers better mileage. However, check these Packards for abnormal front-end rake induced by tired springs caused by supporting this relatively heavy engine.

Superchargers are always worth a check by an expert. The variable-ratio McCulloch blowers sometimes exhibit pulley spline wear and bearing failure.

Production

Town Sedan	3,940
Country Sedan	869

Identification

Obvious Studebaker body shell with sharply peaked front fenders, 1956 Clipper wheel covers and taillights, 1956 Packard script, 1955 Packard hood ornament. Supercharged V-8 engine.

Specifications

Engine: Overhead-valve V-8, 289 ci (3.56 x 3.63 in.), supercharged, 275 bhp.

Wheelbase: 120.5 in. on Town Sedan, 116.5 in. on Country Sedan.

Chassis and drivetrain: Independent front suspension with coil springs and tubular shocks; live rear axle with semi-elliptic leaf springs. Flightomatic transmission standard. Curb weight 3,570 lb. on Town Sedan, 3,650 lb. on Country Sedan.

Serial Numbers

57L L1001 to 57L L5809

Price History

95+ point condition 1	1982	1987	1992	Return
Town Sedan	$2,750	$5,000	$6,000	16.9%
Country Sedan	3,000	5,500	7,500	20.1

The Country Sedan version of the 1957 Packard Clipper was a good-looking station wagon and the first of that body style since 1950. Using another Studebaker body, the wagon had a shorter wheelbase than the sedan. Collectors need to check floors, rocker panels and fenders for tinworm, which is rampant on these cars.

Chapter 27

Packard, 1958

Hawk, Hardtop, Sedan and Station Wagon

	Fun	Investment	Anguish
Hawk	9	9	5
Hardtop	6	6	5
Sedan	4	4	5
Station Wagon	4	5	5

Last of the marque, a quartet of Studebaker-based Packards closed out a history dating to the nineteenth century and left everyone who loves cars poorer, though few say they were poorer for the loss of the 1958 Packards. Overstyled, largely by Duncan McRae under the aegis of Curtiss-Wright president Roy Hurley, the 1958s were an example of trying to keep up with current competitive designs on a shoestring budget. Interestingly, McRae, a car enthusiast, managed to retain the outline of the famous Packard hood on all four cars—one final nod to a glorious past.

Keeping up with the competition required some strange operations. On the non-Hawk models, it was necessary to graft quad headlamps to three models—in no way could these be plastered on the Hawk or they would have done it. Also, because the public liked tailfins, McRae was asked to double the count—the 1957 Packard fins were shrouded by another pair, welded right over them. A gold sweepspear along the body sides and

The 1958 Packard Hardtop was based on Studebaker's concurrent Starlight, a one-year-only model which was scrubbed in 1959 owing to Studebaker's shift to Lark production and the demise of Packard. Hex wheel covers and ox-yoke sculpting around the grille continued the traditional images.

smaller, 14 in. wheels were other popular fetishes of the times.

The 1958 Packard Station Wagon (spelled with capital letters now) had a nine-passenger option involving a rear-facing back seat. A nicer-looking model was the Hardtop, with a striking roofline, sharing its body with two Studebaker hardtops called Starliners (the Packard version had no special name). Least attractive was the four-door sedan, which just looked ugly.

The Packard Hawk materialized because Hurley had admired the Mercedes-Benz 300SL in Germany and asked McRae to conjure one up; wags dubbed the prototype the "Hurley Hawk," and not until very late did the McRae realize it was going into production.

The basis of the Packard Hawk was the Studebaker Golden Hawk 400, an upper-crust trim variation of the sporty Studebaker with a beautiful full-leather interior. Like the Golden Hawk, the Packard Hawk carried an engine-turned metal dashboard, supercharged V–8, stand-up fender-mounted parking lights and big, concave tailfins. To give Packard's version a different look, McRae created a huge, blacked-out oval

Leftover Clipper wheel covers were pressed into service for the last of the marque. *George Hamlin*

grille, in which the front bumper more or less floated. He also smoothed-off the deck and topped it with a spare-tire outline. Inspired by classic aircraft, he finished the Hawk off with pleated vinyl armrests along the beltline. Whereas the wagon and hardtop rode Studebaker's 116.5 in. wheelbase, the Hawk and Packard Sedan were on a 120.5 in. wheelbase.

The most collectible 1958 Packard is the Hawk, with production of only 588. It was Packard's version of the Studebaker Golden Hawk 400 and the only supercharged model in the 1958 Packard line. Full-leather interior, beltline padding that resembled classic aircraft and gold Mylar-covered concave tailfins were identifying characteristics.

Going one tailfin up on the competition, stylist Duncan McRae tacked on high-altitude dorsals when told to make the 1958 look different on a negligible budget. TT badge on deck signifies Studebaker's Twin Traction or positive-lock differential. *George Hamlin*

A trace of the 1955–1956 Packard dash remained on the 1958s, but the horn button bore Studebaker-Packard's hawk emblem instead of the Packard coat of arms. *George Hamlin*

Studebaker-Packard had successfully given the 1958 Packard its own personality, despite its obvious Studebaker origins. Contrary to popular belief, these modifications and the Packard name did not imply a higher price; except with the Hawk, in fact, the comparable Studebaker President actually cost more:

Make	Hawk	Hardtop	Sedan	Wagon
Packard	$3,995	$3,262	$3,212	$3,555
Studebaker	3,470	3,355	3,365	NA

The problem was that people weren't buying Studebakers, either.

By midsummer 1958, the decision was made not to build another Packard automobile, ersatz or real, at least in the immediate future. Studebaker-Packard was now staking its future on the compact Lark, scheduled to debut later in the year as a 1959 model. Though the Lark saved the company for a time, it was not enough in the end.

The Packard name was dropped from the corporate title in 1962. American production of Studebakers stopped in December 1963, and the last Studebakers were 1966 models built in Canada.

Thus with these 1958 models, the grand old name of Packard reached the end of its history.

What To Look For

The Packard Hawk is head and shoulders above the other 1958 models in collector esteem, and is the only one of the four being seriously collected by Packard, as opposed to Studebaker, enthusiasts. This has to do with its outstanding performance (it's the only supercharged 1958 model), its beautiful leather interior and its quirky exterior, which seems to look better in light colors. Unlike the Golden Hawk 400, which was extremely scarce even when new, the Packard Hawk is in relatively good supply, since most of the 588 examples were saved with the knowledge that they were among the last Packards. Which model is actually *the* last is not known, because serial numbers were used indiscriminately between body styles.

Among non-Hawks, the Hardtop is the most desirable, despite the extreme rarity of the Station Wagon, which nevertheless has not gone up in price as fast as comparable cars with low production figures.

On all models, look for completeness; trim parts exclusive to these cars are in short supply. The Packard Hawk is ironically the easiest restoration, since its all-leather interior can be easily replicated. Buyers should acquire fine restored or original examples of the non-Hawk models, because the cost of restoration is not presently warranted by market value.

Problem Areas

Exactly the same problems affect the 1958s as the 1957s. Rust is the number-one malady. It starts on the front fenders but quickly spreads to the floors, trunk, wheel arches and rocker panels. Buy a car that has spent its life in a rustfree zone if you can, and invest in expert rustproofing.

The Studebaker drivetrain is reliable, and the 289 V–8 both supercharged and normally aspirated is reliable and long-lived. It is a heavy engine, and like the 1957s, 1958 models should be checked for abnormal front-end rake induced by tired springs.

The Hawk's superchargers should be examined carefully, since they sometimes exhibit pulley spline wear and bearing failure.

Fewer than 200 1958 wagons were built. Quad headlamps, found on all 1958 Packards except the Hawk, were grafted on after competitive pressure convinced the company that they were needed. In retrospect, they needn't have bothered.

Identification

Quad headlamps and double tailfins using 1956–1957 Clipper taillights on all models except the Hawk. Full-leather interior, vinyl beltline padding, concave gold Mylar covering outside of tailfins, Studebaker taillights. Hawk has supercharged engine, wide black oval grille with floating bumper and spare tire on deck.

Serial Numbers

Hawk: 58L LS–101 to 58L LS–688
Other models: 58L L101 to 58L L L1889
Body designations:
Hawk: K9
Sedan: Y8
Hardtop: J8
Station Wagon: P8

Production

Model	Total
Sedan	1,200
Hardtop	675
Hawk	588
Station Wagon	159

Specifications

Model	Bore x Stroke	CI	Bhp	Wheelbase
Hawk	3.56 x 3.63 in.	289	275	120.5 in.
Sedan	3.56 x 3.63	289	225	120.5
Hardtop and Station Wagon	3.56 x 3.63	289	225	116.5

Chassis and drivetrain: Independent front suspension with coil springs and tubular shocks; live rear axle with semi-elliptic leaf springs. Flightomatic transmission standard. Curb weight 3,470 lb. on Hawk, 3,505 lb. on Sedan, 3,480 lb. on Hardtop, 3,750 lb. on Station Wagon.

Bodies: Four-door sedan, four-door station wagon, two-door hardtop.

Price History

95+ point condition 1	1982	1987	1992	Return
Hawk	$6,000	$11,000	$17,500	23.9%
Hardtop	4,000	7,000	10,000	20.1
Sedan	3,000	5,500	6,500	16.7
Station Wagon	3,500	6,250	8,000	18.0

Chapter 28

Professional Packards

Funeral, Rescue, Livery and Commercial Vehicles

The collection, preservation and exhibition of professional cars—specialized vehicles for funeral, rescue or livery work, converted by a custom-body firm but based on passenger car styling—has only recently become significant, as has the collection of trucks. Both these fields are now burgeoning.

Body styles included in the definition of professional cars are hearses, ambulances, service cars, limousines, sedans with extra seating and flower cars. In the North American industry, vehicles such as these often shared common tooling, and the whole line of bodies was offered by larger manufactur-

A Henney display in 1948 features a smartly executed ambulance. In the background were a standard Custom Eight and a Henney Packard hearse.

ers such as Hess & Eisenhardt of Ohio, Henney of Illinois or Armbruster Stageway of Arkansas. Commonality of tooling, in fact, also produced a number of combination vehicles that fit into the definition of a professional car: hearse-ambulance, sedan-ambulance, even hearse-limousine. Such cars can be converted from one use to another in minutes by cleverly designed seating and equipment hardware.

Although these vehicles were neither plentiful nor useful as family transport after retirement, they were generally of quality craftsmanship and thus were occasionally picked up and preserved by collectors—usually as a sideline to collecting more conventional body styles. More often, however, they fell prey to the scrappers, surfers and part-outers, who would take one or two near-mint trim items and discard the remainder of the car. Such wasteful practices were encouraged by the low price of retired professional cars (funeral homes and ambulance services had no need for old units) and by the unwillingness of the large car clubs to allow the cars (other than limousines) into exhibition.

From the mid-1970s to the early 1990s this picture changed significantly. The rise of ambulance-preservation societies, and a few hearse and ambulance appreciation groups in various parts of the world, led eventually to the formation of the Professional Car Society. Eventually, the existence

A 1953 Henney Junior ambulance owned by George Hamlin is a prominent part of many Packard Club National meets and events hosted by Mid-Atlantic Packards, whose name it carries.

of the PCS and the voices of other collectors coaxed the Antique Automobile Club of America into trying an ambulance classification, and later a class for hearses, in its display rules. Whereas most of the professional car collecting up to 1980 was done by isolated individuals, funeral directors and rescue squads, these cars are now more commonly found in the ranks of club rosters, and judging classifications exist for them at large shows. These trends seem likely to continue.

Professional Packards have always been a significant part of this market, both as new

A Packard Super long-wheelbase car from the factory archives. Whether any were actually built in this form for taxi or livery use is questionable.

cars and as collectible cars. In the early days of the motor hearse and the motorized ambulance, the Packard chassis offered what many others did not and what were considered indispensable in these markets: dependability, dignity and performance. An anemic ambulance would not serve a patient well; a noisy hearse detracted from the ceremony in which it was taking part. A car that did not start every time served neither purpose. Thus many shops making these specialized bodies designed them for Packard chassis. Many customers specified it.

Early industry practice favored the "assembled" chassis, or one that the manufacturer built up out of parts sourced industrywide. The assembled car was marketed as an "own make" and had its own front end and grille design. Leaders in this practice included Hess & Eisenhardt, Cunningham and Henney. Hess & Eisenhardt, in fact, continued to market its own make into the 1940s, even after it stopped using a different grille and it became obvious that the base chassis was, say, a LaSalle with extra grille stripes.

As some marques gained reputation and others lost it, customers began to favor the "manufactured" chassis. The fronts all looked the same and were identifiable as to make, but the bodies could come from a dozen firms. Packard was the favorite chassis used in the making of manufactured-chassis professional cars. The process generally involved stretching the frame.

Fortunately, Packard realized that it could best serve this market by offering a long-wheelbase chassis designed for the professional car builders. Such a chassis would minimize mechanical customization and attract the widest range of body firms. Such special chassis were designated with an A suffix and, with the advent of the One Twenty in 1935, made a significant impact on the body industry with the 120A version. Industry leaders like Miller, Henney, Silver-Knightstown, Cunningham, Eureka, Meteor and Superior rushed to offer bodies on the 120A and companion chassis in the Eight, Super Eight and even Twelve lines.

Eventually, however, Packard became convinced that it could best protect its name and the engineering integrity of its products by concentrating on a single body maker. It chose the industry leader, Henney of Freeport, Illinois. By a contract signed in 1936, Packard agreed to supply chassis to no other body firm, and although Henney was under no similar constraint, it generally confined its work to Packards from then until 1954.

The agreement did not guarantee either firm long life. Henney ceased operations

Henney Packard funeral car: a sketch from the Packard archives, apparently done in 1953

(note the taillights) despite the 1951–style front end—or airbrushed to update an earlier sketch.

during 1954 following a series of financial crises similar to those about to befall Packard. As a result, however, the vast majority of professional Packards are likely to be Henneys, and not only the obvious hearses, ambulances and flower cars, but also the limousines and seven-passenger sedans of 1946–1947 (which have no body maker identified anywhere on them) and of 1953–1954 (which have a small Henney plate discreetly hidden on the inside doorjamb).

Collectors pondering a professional Packard have a wide range of body styles and makers to choose from. The one make that probably qualifies as "The Universal Car" is the long-wheelbase limousine and sedan of 1946–1947. These cars share many components with the stock Custom Super Clipper four-door sedans, but they are higher and, of course, longer. They are universal because they are eligible for nearly every major club and show under the sun, qualifying as each of the following: Packards, welcome at every Packard meet; professional cars, with entree to the Professional Car Society; Classics, among the few post-World War II cars recognized by the Classic Car Club of America; Milestones, recognized by the Milestone Car Society as outstanding postwar cars; antiques, old enough for antique car shows including those sponsored by the Antique Automobile Club of America; veterans, eligible through their Milestone status for events of the Veteran Motor Car Club of America.

No other car is so eligible; indeed, these Henney Packards can even be taken to events sponsored by the Studebaker Drivers Club, a nod to the days when Studebaker and Packard shared corporate offices.

What To Look For

Production quantities of the long-wheelbase Clipper were on the order of 3,000, but more limited numbers were normal. In a particular year only a few hundred professional Packards may have been built, and if the idea is to find something like an airport limousine or a flower car, the production was so small—a handful a year—as to make the search a real snipe hunt.

No factory support is available, but neither is it available for any other older professional car, because every company active in Packard's last decade has failed or been sold except one. Even where the name remains—say, Superior—it is not the *same* firm. The sole remaining company still doing business as itself—Hess & Eisenhardt—sold off its Sayers & Scoville arm years ago and now deals only in specialty limousines. In the course of such corporate upheaval, things like records, drawings, parts and fabric samples have a way of being lost.

Resale values of professional Packards are usually less than those of other body styles because of the storage problems and limited use. A typical Packard hearse weighs 6,000 lb., takes 22 ft. of garage space or more, barely clears the overhead and seats only two . . . or one more laying down.

Limited appeal means that this class of vehicle is more affordable to start on than, say, a dual cowl phaeton. The challenges of restoring a professional Packard are usually worth it, moreover because the finished result is at once the longest and most eye-catching vehicle in the class in which it parks at a meet or show.

With any professional car, the main thing to beware of is mechanical abuse. Hearses were frequently driven at slow speeds and shut off cold. Ambulances were often driven recklessly, or shut off cold, or run at idle for hours or launched at high speeds before oil pressure was up. An absolutely gorgeous car may be in serious need of engine or transmission work.

Body parts were made by specialty firms such as Henney, and many equivalent passenger-car parts, like rear bumpers, will not interchange. The curved glass of the 1951–1954 models is unique and will probably never be reproduced. The heavier weight of the professional cars has apparently resulted in an abnormal rate of axle failure; the cognoscenti carry an extra rear axle, with bearing installed, everywhere they go.

Packard Trucks

The Packard truck, built from an indeterminant year in the early 1900s through 1923, represents an interesting challenge for the collector. Everything on it is scarce. However, a clearinghouse, the Packard Truck Organization, exists, and some items are being reproduced. Of no small help is the coincidence that the Goodyear Tire and Rubber Company maintains a Packard truck, the Wingfoot Express, for advertising, and campaigns it heavily.

Tires are a major problem. Though pneumatics for the later models are now available thanks to Goodyear, solid tires for the early trucks have to be built individually. Add the building of new wooden spoke wheels (repairing bad ones is impossible) and you have a large bill; lots of owners have changed to disc wheels, but only so many of them are available.

Radiator repair is a common project. These trucks when new were used for heavy jobs on rough surfaces with rock-solid suspensions. The brass honeycomb radiators on the larger models simply could not take the vibration. On the other hand, the mechanical aspects of the Packard truck are straightforward and present no significant or insurmountable challenges.

Clubs and Rosters

Eastern Packard Club, Inc., PO Box 153, Fairfield, CT 06430. Founded to supplement the work of the two large American clubs and as a focus for Packard enthusiasts in the Northeast. Publication includes 8x10 in. commercial black-and-white photos of members' cars. About 350 members; dues are $20 per year.

Old Dominion Packard Club, PO Box 1702, West Point, VA 23181. Independent regional organization with an active program of events. Holds two meeting per year and publishes a periodic newsletter. About 120 members; dues are $8 per year.

The Packard Club, Inc. (Packard Automobile Classics), PO Box 2808, Oakland, CA 94618. The world's largest Packard club, with thirty-six regions sponsoring numerous events annually and an annual convention that rotates around the United States. Publishes a quarterly magazine and monthly news bulletin. About 3,500 members; dues are $30 per year.

Packards England, 13 Underlane, Plympton, Plymouth, Devon, United Kingdom PL7 3QU. The United Kingdom affiliate of The Packard Club, with numerous members and activities in southern England.

Packards International Motor Car Club, 302 French Street, Santa Ana, CA 92701. Another major national Packard club with a dozen regions sponsoring local events, a quarterly magazine and a periodical bulletin. About 2,000 members; dues are $25 per year.

Packard Truck Organization, 1196 Mountain Road, York Springs, PA 17372. Open to owners of Packard trucks, offering an interchange of vital information on restoration and parts sources among members, as well as a quarterly publication. Packard truck owners should send four long self-addressed stamped envelopes with postage for two ounces affixed to each. Thirty-four members; dues are $5 per year.

Packard Twin Six Organization, PO Box 24125, Oklahoma City, OK 73124. Serves as a register and cars and parts interchange for owners of 1932–1939 Packard Twin Sixes and Twelves. Ownership is required for membership; no dues.

PAC Australia, PO Box 14, Turramurra, New South Wales, Australia 2074. A large and active Australian club, with many events throughout Australia and a periodical.

Antique Automobile Club of America, 501 W. Governor Road, PO Box 417, Hershey, PA 17033. Welcomes all Packard cars. Is the world's largest old-car organization. 50,000 members; dues are $18 per year.

Classic Car Club of America, 2300 E. Devon Avenue, Suite 126, Des Plaines, IL 60018. Welcomes all Packards cited as Classics from the period 1925–1947. About 5,000 members; dues are $30 per year.

Contemporary Historical Vehicle Association, 16944 Dearborn Street, Sepulveda, CA 91343. Recognizes all Packards since 1928. About 2,200 members; dues are $15 per year.

Milestone Car Society, PO Box 55013, Indianapolis, IN 46205. Recognizes all Packards cited as Milestones from the period 1946–1956. About 1,000 members; dues are $25 per year.

Professional Car Society, PO Box 09636, Columbus, OH 43209. Dedicated to the maintenance and preservation of all years and makes of professional cars. Distributes a quarterly publication. About 500 members; dues are $15 per year.

Veteran Motor Car Club of America, PO Box 360788, Strongsville, OH 44136. Recognizes pre-World War II Packards and post-World War II models cited as Milestones. About 7,000 members; dues are $30 per year.

Rosters

1899–1958 Packard Dealers
Ken Chapman
602 S. Franklin Street
Farmington, MO 63640

1899–1903 Warren, Ohio, Era
Models A, B, C, E, F, G, K, M
Terry Martin
380 Fairmount Drive, NE
Warren, OH 44483

1904–1923 Packard Trucks
David Lockard
1196 Mountain Road
York Springs, PA 17372

1907–1912 Four Cylinder
Model Thirty and Eighteen
Mrs. Howard G. Henry
500 Piney Creek Lane
North East, MD 21901

1912–1915 Dominant Six
All Model 38s and 48s
Don E. Weber
1100 NE Loop 410, #636
San Antonio, TX 78209

1920–1922 First Series Single Six
Model 116
Dan Liebermann
2728 Benvenue Avenue
Berkeley, CA 94705

1920–1923 First Series Single Six
Models 116, 126, 133
Mike Tedrake
1240 Cobridge Drive
Rochester, MI 48064

1925–1926 Third Series Six
Models 326, 333
Chris Strathopulo
1402 Cherokee Trail
Plano, TX 75023

1928 Fifth Series Six
Models 526, 533
Grover J. Secord
6442 Patmore Road
Memphis, TN 38134

1928 Fourth Series Eight
Model 443
George Townsend
201 Nale Drive
Madison, AL 35758

1930 Seventh Series Standard Eight
Model 733
Don Cockburn
49 Toynbee Trail
West Hill, Ontario
M1E 1G1 Canada

1930 Seventh Series Custom and Deluxe Eight
Models 740, 745
Bill Scorah
POBox 30281, Uptown Station
Albuquerque, NM 87190

1930 Seventh Series Speedsters
Model 734
Bruce Grinager
8836 Willoughby Road
Pittsburgh, PA 15237

1931 Eighth Series Standard, Custom, DeLuxe Eight
Models 826, 833, 840, 845
Bob Turnquist
POBox 56
Morristown, NJ 07960

1931–1939 Eighth-Seventeenth Series
  Packard Motor Car Co. of Canada, Ltd.
All models built in Canada
David Knight
421 Upper Kenilworth Avenue
Hamilton, Ontario, L8T 4G7 Canada

1932 Ninth Series Light Eight
Model 900
Jeffery Hammers
Penn-Dutch Restorations
4 Commerce Drive
Glen Rock, PA 17327

1932 Ninth Series Twin Six
Models 905, 906
C. A. Leslie, Jr.
POBox 24125
Oklahoma City, OK 73124

1932–1939 Ninth-Seventeenth Series Twin
  Six and Twelve
Models 905, 906, 1005, 1006, 1106, 1107,
  1108, 1206, 1207, 1208, 1406, 1407,
  1408, 1506, 1507, 1508, 1607, 1608,
  1707, 1708
Charles A. Blackman
4409 Dobie Road
Okemos, MI 48864

1933–1934 Tenth and Eleventh Series
  Eight and Super Eight
Models 1001, 1002, 1003, 1004, 1100,
  1101, 1102, 1103, 1104, 1105
James Pearsall
POBox 128
Zarephath, NJ 08890

1934 Eleventh Series Eight and Super
  Eight
Models 1100, 1101, 1102, 1103, 1104, 1105
Haden Vandiver
POBox 333
Alvarado, TX 76009

1934 Eleventh Series Super Eight Sport
  Phaeton
Model 1104–761
Robert V. Russell
Rt. 3, Box 3153
Clayton, GA 30525

1934 Eleventh Series Twelve

Models 1106, 1107, 1108
Edward Blend
802 Eighth Street
Irwin, PA 15642

1935 Twelfth Series Eight 127 in. Four-
  Door Sedan
Model 1200–803
Michael Barnes
1712 Dutchess Avenue
Dayton, OH 45420

1935–1936 Twelfth and Fourteenth Series
  Eight and Super Eight
Models 1200, 1201, 1202, 1203, 1204, 1205,
  1400, 1401, 1402, 1403, 1404, 1405
L. Michael Corbin
RD 2, Box 110–K
Dagsboro, DE 19939

1935–1937 Twelfth-Fifteenth Series
  LeBaron Town Cars
Models 194–195, 294–295, L–394, L–395
Bob Supina
901 Cowart Creek Drive
Friendswood, TX 77546

1936–1937 Fourteenth and Fifteenth Series
  One Twenty Convertible Sedan
Models 120–B–997, 120–C–1097
Phil Baumgarten
277 SW 33rd Court
Ft. Lauderdale, FL 33315–3340

1937 Fifteenth Series Six
Model 115–C
Kevin Rice
3174 White Tail Lane
Adel, IA 50003–9724

1937 Fifteenth Series One Twenty
Models 120–C, 120–CD, 138–CD, except
  convertible sedan and station wagon
Bob Zale
2331 Valencia Terrace
Charlotte, NC 28226

1937 Fifteenth Series Super Eight and
  Twelve
Models 1500, 1501, 1502, 1506, 1507, 1508
Bob Supina
901 Cowart Creek Drive
Friendswood, TX 77546

1937–1941 Fifteenth-Nineteenth Series
  Station Wagons
Charles A. Blackman
4409 Dobie Road
Okemos, MI 48864

1938 Sixteenth Series Six
Model 1600
Rob Evans
1701 Williams Street #C
Valdosta, GA 31602

1938 Sixteenth Series Super Eight
Models 1603, 1604, 1605
Arthur James
155 Col. Danforth Trail
West Hill, Ontario
M1C 1P8 Canada

1938–1939 Sixteenth and Seventeenth Ser-
  ies Twelve
Models 1607, 1608, 1707, 1708
Bonnie Franko
724 Shanlee Drive
Webster, NY 14580

1939 Seventeenth Series Six
Model 1700
Scott H. Bell
1111 Army Navy Drive #B–407
Arlington, VA 22202

1940–1941 Eighteenth-Nineteenth Series
  One Ten, One Twenty, Clipper, Super
  Eight One Sixty, 1942 Twentieth Series
  Six Special, Six Custom, Eight Special,
  Eight Custom, Super Eight One Sixty
Models 1800, 1801, 1803, 1804, 1805,
  1900, 1902, 1903, 1904, 1905, 1951,
  2000, 2001, 2003, 2004, 2005, 2010,
  2011, 2020, 2021, 2023, 2030
J.P. McVicker
3031 Hunt Road
Oakton, VA 22124

1940 Eighteenth Series Darrin 700 and 710
Models 1801, 1806, 1807
Eugene Tareshawty
11 Colonial Drive
Youngstown, OH 44505

1940 Eighteenth Series Custom Super

Eight, One Eighty Touring and Division
  Window Limousines
Model 1808–1350
Marshall Katz
246 N. 32nd Street
Camp Hill, PA 17011

1940–1942 Eighteenth-Twentieth Series
  Custom Super Eight One Eighty
Models 1806, 1807, 1808, 1906, 1907,
  1908, 2006, 2007, 2008
Charles A. Blackman
4409 Dobie Road
Okemos, MI 48864

1941–1947 Nineteenth-Twenty-first Series
  Clipper
Models 1951, 2000, 2001, 2003, 2006,
  2010, 2011, 2100, 2101, 2103, 2106,
  2111, 2120, 2130
Steve Chapman
1602 Alexander
Waxahachie, TX 75165

1942 Twentieth Series Convertible Coupe
  and Darrin
Models 1529, 1579, 1589, 1599
A.H. Rohlfing
15 Leeuwarden Lane
Darien, CT 06820

1942–1947 Twentieth and Twenty-first
  Series Clipper Custom Super Eight Club
  Sedan
Models 2006–1525, 2106–1625, 2106–2125
Martin S. Cousineau
1301 Woodruff Avenue
Los Angeles, CA 90024–5129

1946–1947 Twenty-first Series Custom
  Super Eight Lwb Seven-Pass. and
  Limousine
Models 1650, 1651, 2150, 2152
Charles A. Blackman
4409 Dobie Road
Okemos, MI 48864

1948–1949 Twenty-second and Twenty-
  third Series Super Eight 141 in. Seven-
  Passenger and Limousine
Models 2222, 2222–9, 2322
Tommy Baccaro

12122 Kirkholm
Houston, TX 77089

1948–1950 Twenty-second and Twenty-
third Series
Models 2201, 2202, 2206, 2211, 2213,
2220, 2222, 2225, 2232, 2233, 2240,
2301, 2302, 2306, 2313, 2320, 2322,
2332, 2333
John P. Northrup
1948 West Barron Road
Howell, MI 48843

1948–1950 Twenty-second and Twenty-
third Series Convertible
Models 2259, 2279, 2359, 2379
Stella Pyrtek-Blond
84 Hoy Avenue
Fords, NJ 08863

1948–1950 Twenty-second and Twenty-
third Series Henney Packard
Dale K. Cole
784 Wilwood
Rochester Hills, MI 48309

1951–1952 Twenty-fourth and Twenty-
fifth Series
Models 2401, 2402, 2406, 2413, 2501,
2502, 2506, 2513, 2531
Ed Ostrowski
145 Worrin Road
Shenfield, Brentwood
Essex, England CM15 8JR

1951–1954 Factory Experimental
All Pan Americans, Panthers, etc.
Dwight R. Heinmuller
16529 Dubbs Road
Sparks, MD 21152

1951–1956 Custom Body
All Derhams, Henneys, etc.
Peter Grave
POBox 175
Ottsville, PA 18942

1953 Twenty-sixth Series
All models except Caribbean Models 2601,
2602, 2606, 2611, 2613, 2626, 2631, 2633
George Papageorge, Jr.
37680 Lincoln Trail
North Branch, MN 55056

1953 Twenty-sixth Series Mayfair Hardtop
Model 2677
David B. Rietz
1682 Clifton Avenue
Highland Park, IL 60035

1953 Twenty-sixth Series Patrician Sedan
Model 2652
Kent W. Trimble
3447 52nd Street Court
Moline, IL 61265–6628

1953 Convertible
Model 2679
Steve Strack
4204 Glenridge Street
Kensington, MD 20895

1953–1954 Twenty-sixth and Fifty-fourth
Series Caribbean
Models 2678, 5478
Lee Stewart
605 Greenridge
Longview, TX 75601

1954 Fifty-fourth Series with 359 Engine
Models 5450, 5451, 5452, 5477, 5478, 5479
Keith Vail
302 Monticello Avenue
Salisbury, MD 21801

1955–1956 Packard and Clipper
Models 5540, 5560, 5580, 5640, 5660,
5670A, 5680, 5688
Stuart R. Blond
84 Hoy Avenue
Fords, NJ 08863

1955–1956 Caribbean
Models 5588, 5697, 5699
Peter Grave
POBox 175
Ottsville, PA 18942

1958 Packard Hawk
Model K–8
LaFayette Keaton
3540 Mississippi Avenue
Portland, OR 97227–1155

Publications

Books

Packard: A History of the Motorcar and the Company, by numerous authors. New York, E.P. Dutton, 1978. The ultimate history of Packard, and the one book to have if you can own only one, as far as Packards are concerned.

The Packard Story, by Robert Turnquist. Reprinted 1975. One of the first marque histories on any car, and still a valuable source of information, particularly about Packards from 1925–1942. Available from Classic Cars Inc., see Parts and Services section following.

Standard Catalog of American Cars 1805–1942, edited by Henry Austin Clark, Jr., and Beverly Rae Kimes. Iola, WI, Krause Publications, 1985. The most comprehensive source of facts and figures on cars of the period.

Standard Catalog of American Cars 1946–1975, edited by John Gunnell. Second revised edition. Iola, WI, Krause Publications, 1987. The post-World War II equivalent of the 1805–1942 catalog.

Used Car Value Guide, published by the National Automobile Dealers Association. Detroit, 1954 and 1958. An excellent source of model and body style lineups and contemporary used car values.

Red Book used car value guides, 1932 and 1935. Reprinted facsimile editions. Minneapolis, Motorbooks International, 1970. Similar in format to the *Used Car Value Guides* covering pre-World War II makes and models.

Periodicals

The Packard Cormorant. I have cited the journal I have edited and published for The Packard Club since 1975 to assist the reader in finding further information, but also to pay tribute to the many people who have contributed their historical and technical expertise on Packards over the years. Most copies are still in print. Copies of the numbers cited in this book may be obtained from the publisher at $5 per issue postpaid: Dragonwyck Publishing, Inc., PO Box 385-C, Hopkinton, NH 03229.

The Cormorant. This was the name by which the above journal was known through 1975. Unfortunately, back issues are not available.

Parts and Services

A&M Garage
2651 Webster Avenue
Bronx, NY 10458
    Parts for circa 1953–1958 Packards.

American Arrow Corporation
105 Kinross
Clawson, MI 48017
    Mascots, wire wheels, windwings,
    tonneau windshields, luggage rack strips,
    Packard-Hall spotlights, mirrors, badge
    bars.

Autosport Packard
PO Box 9553
Knoxville, TN 379409
    Umbrellas, key fobs, hats, jackets with
    Packard regalia.

Bellevue Hotel
15 E. Street NW
Washington, DC 20001
    Special rates for Packard club members,
    free pickup in Packard limousine at
    Union Station or any airport. Premises
    feature the Packard Grille, open
    Thursday through Saturday evenings,
    with dealer signs and memorabilia.

Stuart Blond
84 Hoy Avenue
Fords, NJ 08863
    Roster of 1955–1956 Caribbeans. Editor
    of Packard Club *News-Bulletin*.

Brinton's Antique Auto Parts
6826 SW McVey Avenue
Redmond, OR 97756
    Parts for 1920–1932 Six, Eight, Super
    Eight and Twelve.

Classic Cars Inc.
Maple Terrace
Hibernia, NJ 07842
    Packard parts 1925–1942; source for *The
    Packard Story,* by Bob Turnquist and
    reprints of 1930 Speedster catalog.

Custom Auto Service
302 French Street
Santa Ana, CA 92701
    Parts, service and restoration for all
    Packards. Also headquarters of Packards
    International.

Dave's Packard Place
5025 Morgan Avenue S
Minneapolis, MN 55419
    Parts for prewar junior models.

Tom W. Dunaway, Jr.
PO Box 5074
Anderson, SC 29623
    New-old-stock 1930–1948 Trippe
    windshield wiper arms and blades,
    headlights, bulbs, Trippe lights, arms,
    brackets, switches.

James Hill
Box 547
Goodwell, OK 73939

Gaskets, timing chains, taillights, points and other parts for 1935–1954 eight-cylinder Packards; two-color Packard stationery.

Bill Hirsch Auto Parts
396 Littleton Avenue
Newark, NJ 07103
Hubcaps, top material, leather, upholstery fabrics, Wilton carpets, wheel trim rings and other trim for 1925–1958 Packards; also rust preventer paints, gasoline preservative and stabilizer.

John G. Ireland
PO Box 112
Bowmanville, Ontario
Canada L1C 3K8
Used parts for 1951–1954 models.

Kanter Auto Products
76 Monroe Street
Boonton, NJ 07005
Large selection of Packard parts; also carpets, car covers, accessories, leather and so on.

John Kepich Exhaust
7520 Clover
Building 6
Mentor, OH 44061
Stainless steel exhaust systems.

Terry Martin
380 Fairmont Drive NE
Warren, OH 44483
Information and expertise on early single-cylinder Packards.

Max Merritt
PO Box 47096
Indianapolis, IN 46227
Dealer; Studebaker and Packard parts.

J. Morrison Better Cars
117 Third Street
Garden City, NY 11530
Service and restoration, antique and Classic Packards.

Motor Car Restoration and Service

2218 SW Salsbury Avenue
Chehalis, WA 98532
Engine, chassis and body restoration, lacquer painting and detailing, specializing in Packards.

New York Classic Car
2201 Town & Country Plaza
Cazenovia, NY 13035
Restoration shop specializing in Packards.

Oakfield Restorations
1380 Hude Oakfield Road
North Bloomfield, OH 44450
Restoration shop specializing in Packards.

Edward J. Ostrowski
19741 Hickory Leaf Lane
Southfield, MI 48076
Roster of 1951–1954 Packard 250 models.

Packards of Florida
7001 Forst City Road
Orlando, FL 32810
Specialist in 1948–1956 Packard parts.

Patrician Industries
20408 Carlysle
Dearborn, MI 48124
Extensive stock of new and used 1935–1956 parts; springs for all 1935–1958 Packards.

Richard C. Percy
663 Colinet Street
Coquitlam, British Columbia
Canada V3J 4X3
Specialist in 1928–1954 parts; also used and reproduction parts dating back to 1919; Packard literature.

Davis G. Phinney
145 Wood Pond Road
Glastonbury, CT 06033
Restoration advice on Twin Six.

Pulfer and Williams
Forest Road
PO Box 67
Hancock, NH 03449

Manufacturer of emblems, nameplates, handles and reproduction mascots; repairer of cloisonné emblems.

Bradley Skinner
3805 Toledo Road
Bartlesville, OK 74003
Restoration advice on Twin Six.

Small World Press
Hester & Railway
Dundas, MN 55019
Shop manuals and parts books.

W. S. Steiger
4135 Pamona Avenue
Miami, FL 33133
Specialist in Packard parts.

Steve's Studebaker-Packard
2287 Second Street
Napa, CA 94559
Packard services including Torsion-Level suspension and electric shift repairs; parts for 1951–1956 models; Packard car sales.

Robert Turnquist: see Classic Cars Inc.

Don Weber
500 Sandau
Suite 452
San Antonio, TX 78216
Restoration advice and register for 1912–1915 Six.

Index